THE SECON[...] OF GOV[...]
AND A LETTER CONCERNING TOLERATION

DOVER THRIFT EDITIONS

John Locke

DOVER PUBLICATIONS
GARDEN CITY, NEW YORK

DOVER THRIFT EDITIONS

GENERAL EDITOR: PAUL NEGRI
EDITOR OF THIS VOLUME: TOM CRAWFORD

Bibliographical Note

This Dover edition, first published in 2002, is an unabridged republication of the
1956 edition of the texts originally published in 1946 by The Macmillan Company,
New York.

Library of Congress Cataloging-in-Publication Data

Locke, John, 1632–1704.
  [Essay concerning the true original extent and end of civil government]
  The second treatise of government ; and, A letter concerning toleration / John
Locke.
     p. cm.
  Edited with an introduction by J.W. Gough.
  "An unabridged republication of the 1956 edition of the texts originally published
in 1946 by the Macmillan Company, New York"—T.p. verso.
  ISBN-13: 978-0-486-42464-4
  ISBN-10: 0-486-42464-2

  1. Political science—Early works to 1800. 2. Liberty—Early works to 1800.
3. Toleration—Early works to 1800. I. Title: Second treatise of government ; and,
A letter concerning toleration. II. Gough, J. W. (John Wiedhofft) III. Locke, John,
1632–1704. Epistola de tolerantia. English. IV. Title: Letter concerning toleration.
V. Title.

JC153 .L85 2002
320'.01—dc21

                                                                    2002067317

Manufactured in the United States of America
42464213   2021
www.doverpublications.com

Note

ONE OF THE MOST influential political thinkers in Western history, English philosopher John Locke (1632–1704) was largely responsible for codifying and consolidating the principles underlying modern democracies, including that of the United States. In fact, Thomas Jefferson was accused of copying the Declaration of Independence from Locke's *Treatise of Government*. Jefferson denied this, but he was undoubtedly familiar with Locke's *Treatise* and the principles laid out therein, which were in common circulation at the time. Locke's *Treatise* actually comprised two parts: the first was a refutation of Robert Filmer's *Patriarcha*, which defended the divine right of kings. The second, more important, treatise (reprinted here) refuted Hobbesian theories of absolutist government, in favor of government based on the ultimate sovereignty of the people.

While Locke's theories were not especially new or revolutionary, his work united the ideas of a generation or more of political thinkers and laid the foundations for democratic freedoms based on government by consent. For Locke, all men were by nature "free, equal and independent," and were entitled to freedom of thought, freedom of speech, and freedom of worship. Moreover, citizens were to be free from restraint and violence from others, including their own governments. In turn, citizens were expected to comply with the laws, which were necessary to preserve and enlarge freedom.

In sum, Locke claimed that the state exists for the good of mankind, and not the reverse, arguing that political power can only be justified when it is "genuinely for the public good," and when the authority of the ruling body is conditional, not absolute. To help maintain controls on the ruling body, Locke proposed a system of "checks and balances," including the separation of the elected legislative body from the executive power. Moreover, if the government fails to fulfill its obligations to the citizenry, the people have the right to rebel against it.

In *A Letter Concerning Toleration*, Locke pleaded for religious toler-
ance on the grounds that "No man by nature is bound unto any particular church or sect. . . ." Instead, the church member belongs to a
"free and voluntary" society, with its own laws, which must be obeyed
by its adherents, but which laws pertain only to itself. The church has
nothing to do with civil government, and has no inherent power to oppress or destroy churches of differing creeds, or to impose or forbid a
particular liturgy. Persecution produces only superficial compliance in
any case. In Locke's view, there is simply no rational justification for religious intolerance. His arguments, in accord with the rationalist senti-
ment of the age, are widely seen today as the intellectual underpin-
nings of the modern concept of a free church in a free state.

Contents

An Essay Concerning the True Original, Extent
and End of Civil Government

AN ESSAY CONCERNING THE TRUE ORIGINAL, EXTENT AND END OF CIVIL GOVERNMENT

Chapter I

or patriarchical rule
o dictated right & rights

It having been shewn in the foregoing discourse:

1. That Adam had not, either by natural right of fatherhood or by positive donation from God, any such authority over his children, or dominion over the world, as is pretended.

2. That if he had, his heirs yet had no right to it.

3. That if his heirs, there being no law of nature nor positive law of God that determines which is the right heir in all cases that may arise, the right of succession, and consequently of bearing rule, could not have been certainly determined.

4. That if even that had been determined, yet the knowledge of which is the eldest line of Adam's posterity, being so long since utterly lost, that in the races of mankind and families of the world there remains not to one above another the least pretence to be the eldest house, and to have the right of inheritance.

All these premises having, as I think, been clearly made out, it is impossible that the rulers now on earth should make any benefit, or derive any the least shadow of authority from that which is held to be the foundation of all power, Adam's private dominion and paternal jurisdiction; so that he that will not give just occasion to think that all government in the world is the product only of force and violence, and that men live together by no other rules but that of beasts, where the strongest carries it, and so lay a foundation for perpetual disorder and mischief, tumult, sedition, and rebellion (things that the followers of that hypothesis so loudly cry out against), must of necessity find out another rise of government, another original of political power, and another way of designing and knowing the persons that have it, than what Sir Robert Filmer hath taught us.

2. To this purpose, I think it may not be amiss to set down what I take

1

to be political power, that the power of a magistrate over a subject may be distinguished from that of a father over his children, a master over his servant, a husband over his wife, and a lord over his slave. All which distinct powers happening sometimes together in the same man, if he be considered under these different relations, it may help us to distinguish these powers one from another, and shew the difference betwixt a ruler of a commonwealth, a father of a family, and a captain of a galley.

3. Political power, then, I take to be a right of making laws with penalties of death, and consequently all less penalties, for the regulating and preserving of property, and of employing the force of the community in the execution of such laws, and in the defence of the commonwealth from foreign injury; and all this only for the public good.

Chapter II

Of the State of Nature

4. To understand political power aright,[1] and derive it from its original, we must consider what state all men are naturally in, and that is a state of perfect freedom to order their actions and dispose of their possessions and persons as they think fit, within the bounds of the law of nature, without asking leave, or depending upon the will of any other man.

A state also of equality, wherein all the power and jurisdiction is reciprocal, no one having more than another; there being nothing more evident than that creatures of the same species and rank, promiscuously born to all the same advantages of nature, and the use of the same faculties, should also be equal one amongst another without subordination or subjection, unless the Lord and Master of them all should by any manifest declaration of his will set one above another, and confer on him, by an evident and clear appointment, an undoubted right to dominion and sovereignty.

5. This equality of men by nature the judicious Hooker looks upon as so evident in itself and beyond all question, that he makes it the foundation of that obligation to mutual love amongst men on which he builds the duties they owe one another, and from whence he derives the great maxims of justice and charity. His words are:

"The like natural inducement hath brought men to know that it is no less their duty to love others than themselves; for seeing those things

---

1. "Aright" is the reading of the earlier editions, and seems to me preferable to "right," to which it was altered in the collected and later editions.

which are equal must needs all have one measure, if I cannot but wish to receive good, even as much at every man's hands as any man can wish unto his own soul, how should I look to have any part of my desire herein satisfied, unless myself be careful to satisfy the like desire, which is undoubtedly in other men, being of one and the same nature? To have anything offered them repugnant to this desire, must needs in all respects grieve them as much as me, so that, if I do harm, I must look to suffer, there being no reason that others should shew greater measures of love to me than they have by me shewed unto them. My desire, therefore, to be loved of my equals in nature as much as possible may be, imposeth upon me a natural duty of bearing to themward fully the like affection; from which relation of equality between ourselves and them that are as ourselves, what several rules and canons natural reason hath drawn for direction of life no man is ignorant." Eccl. Pol., lib. i.

6. But though this be a state of liberty, yet it is not a state of licence; though man in that state have an uncontrollable liberty to dispose of his person or possessions, yet he has not liberty to destroy himself, or so much as any creature in his possession, but where some nobler use than its bare preservation calls for it. The state of nature has a law of nature to govern it, which obliges every one; and reason, which is that law, teaches all mankind who will but consult it, that, being all equal and independent, no one ought to harm another in his life, health, liberty, or possessions. For men being all the workmanship of one omnipotent and infinitely wise Maker—all the servants of one sovereign Master, sent into the world by his order, and about his business—they are his property, whose workmanship they are, made to last during his, not one another's pleasure; and being furnished with like faculties, sharing all in one community of nature, there cannot be supposed any such subordination among us, that may authorize us to destroy one another, as if we were made for one another's uses, as the inferior ranks of creatures are for ours. Every one, as he is bound to preserve himself, and not to quit his station wilfully, so, by the like reason, when his own preservation comes not in competition, ought he, as much as he can, to preserve the rest of mankind, and may[2] not, unless it be to do justice on an offender, take away or impair the life, or what tends to the preservation of the life, the liberty, health, limb, or goods of another.

7. And that all men may be restrained from invading others' rights, and from doing hurt to one another, and the law of nature be observed, which willeth the peace and preservation of all mankind, the execution of the law of nature is in that state put into every man's hand, whereby

---

2. "May" added in collected edition.

every one has a right to punish the transgressors of that law to such a degree as may hinder its violation. For the law of nature would, as all other laws that concern men in this world, be in vain if there were nobody that, in the state of nature, had a power to execute that law, and thereby preserve the innocent and restrain offenders. And if any one in the state of nature may punish another for any evil he has done, every one may do so. For in that state of perfect equality, where naturally there is no superiority or jurisdiction of one over another, what any may do in prosecution of that law, every one must needs have a right to do.

8. And thus in the state of nature one man comes by a power over another; but yet no absolute or arbitrary power, to use a criminal, when he has got him in his hands, according to the passionate heats or boundless extravagancy of his own will; but only to retribute to him so far as calm reason and conscience dictate what is proportionate to his transgression, which is so much as may serve for reparation and restraint. For these two are the only reasons why one man may lawfully do harm to another, which is that we call punishment. In transgressing the law of nature, the offender declares himself to live by another rule than that of reason and common equity, which is that measure God has set to the actions of men, for their mutual security; and so he becomes dangerous to mankind, the tie which is to secure them from injury and violence being slighted and broken by him. Which, being a trespass against the whole species, and the peace and safety of it, provided for by the law of nature, every man upon this score, by the right he hath to preserve mankind in general, may restrain, or, where it is necessary, destroy things noxious to them, and so may bring such evil on any one who hath transgressed that law, as may make him repent the doing of it, and thereby deter him, and by his example others, from doing the like mischief. And in this case, and upon this ground, every man hath a right to punish the offender, and be executioner of the law of nature.

9. I doubt not but this will seem a very strange doctrine to some men: but before they condemn it, I desire them to resolve me by what right any prince or state can put to death or punish an alien, for any crime he commits in their country. 'Tis certain their laws, by virtue of any sanction they receive from the promulgated will of the legislative, reach not a stranger: they speak not to him, nor, if they did, is he bound to hearken to them. The legislative authority, by which they are in force over the subjects of that commonwealth, hath no power over him. Those who have the supreme power of making laws in England, France, or Holland, are to an Indian but like the rest of the world—men without authority. And, therefore, if by the law of nature every man hath not a power to punish offences against it, as he soberly judges the case to require, I see not how the magistrates of any community can punish an

alien of another country; since in reference to him they can have no more power than what every man naturally may have over another.

10. Besides the crime which consists in violating the law, and varying from the right rule of reason, whereby a man so far becomes degenerate, and declares himself to quit the principles of human nature, and to be a noxious creature, there is commonly injury done to some person or other, and some other man[3] receives damage by his transgression: in which case he who hath received any damage has, besides the right of punishment common to him with other men, a particular right to seek reparation from him that has done it. And any other person, who finds it just, may also join with him that is injured, and assist him in recovering from the offender so much as may make satisfaction for the harm he has suffered.

11. From these two distinct rights—the one of punishing the crime, for restraint and preventing the like offence, which right of punishing is in everybody; the other of taking reparation, which belongs only to the injured party—comes it to pass that the magistrate, who by being magistrate hath the common right of punishing put into his hands, can often, where the public good demands not the execution of the law, remit the punishment of criminal offences by his own authority, but yet cannot remit the satisfaction due to any private man for the damage he has received. That, he who has suffered the damage has a right to demand in his own name, and he alone can remit. The damnified person has this power of appropriating to himself the goods or service of the offender, by right of self-preservation, as every man has a power to punish the crime, to prevent its being committed again, by the right he has of preserving all mankind, and doing all reasonable things he can in order to that end. And thus it is that every man in the state of nature has a power to kill a murderer, both to deter others from doing the like injury, which no reparation can compensate, by the example of the punishment that attends it from everybody, and also to secure men from the attempts of a criminal who, having renounced reason, the common rule and measure God hath given to mankind, hath, by the unjust violence and slaughter he hath committed upon one, declared war against all mankind, and therefore may be destroyed as a lion or a tiger, one of those wild savage beasts with whom men can have no society nor security. And upon this is grounded that great law of nature, "Whoso sheddeth man's blood, by man shall his blood be shed." And Cain was so fully convinced that every one had a right to destroy such a criminal,

---

3. Corrected in 6th edition. Earlier editions read: ". . . injury done, and some person or other, some other man . . ." Collected edition reads: ". . . injury done some person or other, some other man . . ."

that after the murder of his brother he cries out, "Every one that findeth me shall slay me;" so plain was it writ in the hearts of all mankind.

12. By the same reason may a man in the state of nature punish the lesser breaches of that law. It will perhaps be demanded, With death? I answer, Each transgression may be punished to that degree, and with so much severity, as will suffice to make it an ill bargain to the offender, give him cause to repent, and terrify others from doing the like. Every offence that can be committed in the state of nature, may, in the state of nature, be also punished equally, and as far forth as it may, in a commonwealth. For though it would be beside my present purpose to enter here into the particulars of the law of nature, or its measures of punishment, yet it is certain there is such a law, and that, too, as intelligible and plain to a rational creature and a studier of that law as the positive laws of commonwealths; nay, possibly plainer, as much as reason is easier to be understood than the fancies and intricate contrivances of men, following contrary and hidden interests put into words; for so truly are a great part of the municipal laws of countries, which are only so far right as they are founded on the law of nature, by which they are to be regulated and interpreted.

13. To this strange doctrine—*viz.*, That in the state of nature every one has the executive power of the law of nature—I doubt not but it will be objected that it is unreasonable for men to be judges in their own cases, that self-love will make men partial to themselves and their friends: and on the other side, that ill-nature, passion, and revenge will carry them too far in punishing others; and hence nothing but confusion and disorder will follow; and that therefore God hath certainly appointed government to restrain the partiality and violence of men. I easily grant that civil government is the proper remedy for the inconveniences of the state of nature, which must certainly be great where men may be judges in their own case, since 'tis easy to be imagined that he who was so unjust as to do his brother an injury, will scarce be so just as to condemn himself for it. But I shall desire those who make this objection, to remember that absolute monarchs are but men; and if government is to be the remedy of those evils which necessarily follow from men's being judges in their own cases, and the state of nature is therefore not to be endured, I desire to know what kind of government that is, and how much better it is than the state of nature, where one man commanding a multitude has the liberty to be judge in his own case, and may do to all his subjects whatever he pleases, without the least liberty to any one to question or control[4] those who execute his

---

4. Altered in 6th edition. Earlier editions read: ". . . least question or control of those who . . ."

pleasure; and in whatsoever he doth, whether led by reason, mistake, or passion, must be submitted to? Much better it is in the state of nature, wherein men are not bound to submit to the unjust will of another[5]: and if he that judges, judges amiss in his own or any other case, he is answerable for it to the rest of mankind.

14. 'Tis often asked as a mighty objection, Where are, or ever were there, any men in such a state of nature? To which it may suffice as an answer at present: That since all princes and rulers of independent governments all through the world are in a state of nature, 'tis plain the world never was, nor ever will be, without numbers of men in that state. I have named all governors of independent communities, whether they are or are not in league with others. For 'tis not every compact that puts an end to the state of nature between men, but only this one of agreeing together mutually to enter into one community, and make one body politic; other promises and compacts men may make one with another, and yet still be in the state of nature. The promises and bargains for truck, etc., between the two men in the desert island, mentioned by Garcilasso de la Vega in his history of Peru[6]; or between a Swiss and an Indian, in the woods of America, are binding to them, though they are perfectly in a state of nature in reference to one another. For truth and keeping of faith belong to men as men, and not as members of society.

15. To those that say there were never any men in the state of nature, I will not only oppose the authority of the judicious Hooker, Eccl. Pol., lib. i, sect. 10, where he says, "The laws which have been hitherto mentioned," i.e., the laws of nature, "do bind men absolutely, even as they are men, although they have never any settled fellowship, and never any solemn agreement amongst themselves what to do or not to do; but forasmuch as we are not by ourselves sufficient to furnish ourselves with competent store of things needful for such a life as our nature doth desire—a life fit for the dignity of man—therefore to supply those defects and imperfections which are in us, as living single and solely by ourselves, we are naturally induced to seek communion and fellowship with others; this was the cause of men's uniting themselves at first in politic societies," but I moreover affirm that all men are naturally in that state, and remain so, till by their own consents they make themselves members of some politic society; and I doubt not, in the sequel of this discourse, to make it very clear.

---

5. Altered in 6th edition. Earlier editions read: ". . . must be submitted to, which men in the state of nature are not bound to do one to another?"

6. Second state of 1st edition. First state reads: "in Soldania, in or between a Swiss and an Indian . . ."

Chapter III

Of the State of War

16. The state of war is a state of enmity and destruction; and therefore declaring by word or action, not a passionate and hasty, but a sedate, settled design upon another man's life, puts him in a state of war with him against whom he has declared such an intention, and so has exposed his life to the other's power to be taken away by him, or any one that joins with him in his defence and espouses his quarrel; it being reasonable and just I should have a right to destroy that which threatens me with destruction. For by the fundamental law of nature, man being to be preserved as much as possible, when all cannot be preserved, the safety of the innocent is to be preferred; and one may destroy a man who makes war upon him, or has discovered an enmity to his being, for the same reason that he may kill a wolf or a lion; because such men are not under the ties of the common law of reason, have no other rule but that of force and violence, and so may be treated as beasts of prey, those dangerous and noxious creatures that will be sure to destroy him whenever he falls into their power.

17. And hence it is that he who attempts to get another man into his absolute power does thereby put himself into a state of war with him; it being to be understood as a declaration of a design upon his life. For I have reason to conclude that he who would get me into his power without my consent, would use me as he pleased when he had got me there, and destroy me too, when he had a fancy to it; for nobody can desire to have me in his absolute power, unless it be to compel me by force to that which is against the right of my freedom, *i.e.*, make me a slave. To be free from such force is the only security of my preservation; and reason bids me look on him as an enemy to my preservation who would take away that freedom which is the fence to it; so that he who makes an attempt to enslave me, thereby puts himself into a state of war with me. He that in the state of nature would take away the freedom that belongs to any one in that state, must necessarily be supposed to have a design to take away everything else, that freedom being the foundation of all the rest; as he that in the state of society would take away the freedom belonging to those of that society or commonwealth, must be supposed to design to take away from them everything else, and so be looked on as in a state of war.

18. This makes it lawful for a man to kill a thief who has not in the least hurt him, nor declared any design upon his life, any farther than by the use of force so to get him in his power as to take away his money or what he pleases from him; because using force, where he has no

right, to get me into his power, let his pretence be what it will, I have no reason to suppose that he who would take away my liberty would not, when he had me in his power, take away everything else. And therefore it is lawful for me to treat him as one who has put himself into a state of war with me, *i.e.*, kill him if I can; for to that hazard does he justly expose himself, whoever introduces a state of war and is aggressor in it.

19. And here we have the plain difference between the state of nature and the state of war, which however some men have confounded, are as far distant as a state of peace, good will, mutual assistance, and preservation, and a state of enmity, malice, violence, and mutual destruction, are one from another. Men living together according to reason, without a common superior on earth with authority to judge between them, are properly in the state of nature. But force, or a declared design of force, upon the person of another, where there is no common superior on earth to appeal to for relief, is the state of war; and 'tis the want of such an appeal gives a man the right of war even against an aggressor, though he be in society and a fellow-subject. Thus a thief, whom I cannot harm, but by appeal to the law, for having stolen all that I am worth, I may kill, when he sets on to rob me but of my horse or coat; because the law, which was made for my preservation, where it cannot interpose to secure my life from present force, which if lost is capable of no reparation, permits me my own defence, and the right of war, a liberty to kill the aggressor, because the aggressor allows not time to appeal to our common judge, nor the decision of the law, for remedy in a case where the mischief may be irreparable. Want of a common judge with authority puts all men in a state of nature; force without right upon a man's person makes a state of war, both where is, and is not, a common judge.

20. But when the actual force is over, the state of war ceases between those that are in society, and are equally on both sides subjected to the fair determination of the law[1]; because then there lies open the remedy of appeal for the past injury, and to prevent future harm. But where no such appeal is, as in the state of nature, for want of positive laws and judges with authority to appeal to, the state of war once begun continues, with a right to the innocent party to destroy the other whenever he can, until the aggressor offers peace, and desires reconciliation on such

---

1. The first state of the 1st edition reads: ". . . on both sides subject to the judge." §20 then concludes with the words in line 26 on the next page: "And, therefore, in such controversies . . ." to the end of the chapter. The intervening paragraphs were added in a second state, apparently to make up for a passage excised from the first state, in which §21 is missing. See P. A. Laslett, "The 1690 Edition of Locke's *Two Treatises of Government*," in *Trans. Cambridge Bibliographical Soc.* iv (1952), 341–347.

terms as may repair any wrongs he has already done, and secure the innocent for the future. Nay, where an appeal to the law and constituted judges lies open, but the remedy is denied by a manifest perverting of justice and a barefaced wresting of the laws, to protect or indemnify the violence or injuries of some men or party of men, there it is hard to imagine anything but a state of war. For wherever violence is used and injury done, though by hands appointed to administer justice, it is still violence and injury, however coloured with the name, pretences, or forms of law; the end whereof being to protect and redress the innocent, by an unbiassed application of it to all who are under it; wherever that is not *bona fide* done, war is made upon the sufferers, who having no appeal on earth to right them, they are left to the only remedy in such cases, an appeal to heaven.

21. To avoid this state of war (wherein there is no appeal but to heaven, and wherein every the least difference is apt to end, where there is no authority to decide between the contenders) is one great reason of men's putting themselves into society and quitting the state of nature. For where there is an authority, a power on earth, from which relief can be had by appeal, there the continuance of the state of war is excluded, and the controversy is decided by that power. Had there been any such court, any superior jurisdiction on earth, to determine the right between Jephtha and the Ammonites, they had never come to a state of war; but we see he was forced to appeal to heaven. "The Lord, the Judge," says he, "be judge this day between the children of Israel and the children of Ammon" (Judges xi. 27), and then prosecuting and relying on his appeal, he leads out his army to battle. And, therefore, in such controversies, where the question is put, Who shall be judge? it cannot be meant, Who shall decide the controversy? Every one knows what Jephtha here tells us, that "the Lord the Judge" shall judge. Where there is no judge on earth, the appeal lies to God in heaven. That question, then, cannot mean, Who shall judge whether another hath put himself in a state of war with me, and whether I may, as Jephtha did, appeal to heaven in it? Of that I myself can only be judge in my own conscience, as I will answer it at the great day, to the supreme Judge of all men.

Chapter IV

Of Slavery

22. The natural liberty of man is to be free from any superior power on earth, and not to be under the will or legislative authority of man, but

to have only the law of nature for his rule. The liberty of man in society is to be under no other legislative power but that established by consent in the commonwealth; nor under the dominion of any will or restraint of any law, but what that legislative shall enact according to the trust put in it. Freedom then is not what Sir Robert Filmer tells us, O. A.[1] 55, "a liberty for every one to do what he lists, to live as he pleases, and not to be tied by any laws." But freedom of men under government is to have a standing rule to live by, common to every one of that society, and made by the legislative power erected in it; a liberty to follow my own will in all things, where the rule prescribes not; and not to be subject to the inconstant, uncertain, unknown, arbitrary will of another man; as freedom of nature is to be under no other restraint but the law of nature.

23. This freedom from absolute, arbitrary power is so necessary to, and closely joined with, a man's preservation, that he cannot part with it but by what forfeits his preservation and life together. For a man not having the power of his own life cannot by compact, or his own consent, enslave himself to any one, nor put himself under the absolute, arbitrary power of another to take away his life when he pleases. Nobody can give more power than he has himself; and he that cannot take away his own life, cannot give another power over it. Indeed, having by his fault forfeited his own life by some act that deserves death, he to whom he has forfeited it may (when he has him in his power) delay to take it, and make use of him to his own service; and he does him no injury by it. For whenever he finds the hardship of his slavery outweigh the value of his life, 'tis in his power by resisting the will of his master to draw on himself the death he desires.

24. This is the perfect condition of slavery, which is nothing else but the state of war continued between a lawful conqueror and a captive. For if once compact enter between them, and make an agreement for a limited power on the one side, and obedience on the other, the state of war and slavery ceases as long as the compact endures. For, as has been said, no man can by agreement pass over to another that which he hath not in himself, a power over his own life.

I confess we find among the Jews as well as other nations that men did sell themselves; but 'tis plain this was only to drudgery, not to slavery. For it is evident the person sold was not under an absolute, arbitrary, despotical power. For the master could not have power to kill him, at any time, whom at a certain time he was obliged to let go free out of his service; and the master of such a servant was so far from hav-

---

1. i.e., *Observations upon Aristotle's Politics*. The passage referred to is on p. 224 of the edition of Filmer's *Works* in Blackwell's Political Texts.

ing an arbitrary power over his life, that he could not at pleasure so much as maim him, but the loss of an eye or tooth set him free. (Exod. xxi.)

Chapter V

Of Property

25. Whether we consider natural reason, which tells us that men being once born have a right to their preservation, and consequently to meat and drink and such other things as nature affords for their subsistence; or revelation, which gives us an account of those grants God made of the world to Adam, and to Noah and his sons, 'tis very clear that God, as King David says, Psalm cxv. 16, "has given the earth to the children of men," given it to mankind in common. But this being supposed, it seems to some a very great difficulty how any one should ever come to have a property in anything. I will not content myself to answer that if it be difficult to make out property upon a supposition that God gave the world to Adam and his posterity in common, it is impossible that any man but one universal monarch should have any property upon a supposition that God gave the world to Adam and his heirs in succession, exclusive of all the rest of his posterity. But I shall endeavour to shew how men might come to have a property in several parts of that which God gave to mankind in common, and that without any express compact of all the commoners.

26. God, who hath given the world to men in common, hath also given them reason to make use of it to the best advantage of life and convenience. The earth and all that is therein is given to men for the support and comfort of their being. And though all the fruits it naturally produces, and beasts it feeds, belong to mankind in common, as they are produced by the spontaneous hand of nature; and nobody has originally a private dominion exclusive of the rest of mankind in any of them as they are thus in their natural state; yet being given for the use of men, there must of necessity be a means to appropriate them some way or other before they can be of any use or at all beneficial to any particular man. The fruit or venison which nourishes the wild Indian, who knows no enclosure, and is still a tenant in common, must be his, and so his, *i.e.*, a part of him, that another can no longer have any right to it, before it can do any good for the support of his life.

27. Though the earth and all inferior creatures be common to all men, yet every man has a property in his own person; this nobody has any right to but himself. The labour of his body and the work of his

hands we may say are properly his. Whatsoever, then, he removes out of the state that nature hath provided and left it in, he hath mixed his labour with, and joined to it something that is his own, and thereby makes it his property. It being by him removed from the common state nature placed it in, it hath by this labour something annexed to it that excludes the common right of other men. For this labour being the unquestionable property of the labourer, no man but he can have a right to what that is once joined to, at least where there is enough and as good left in common for others.

28. He that is nourished by the acorns he picked up under an oak, or the apples he gathered from the trees in the wood, has certainly appropriated them to himself. Nobody can deny but the nourishment is his. I ask, then, When did they begin to be his? when he digested? or when he ate? or when he boiled? or when he brought them home? or when he picked them up? And 'tis plain, if the first gathering made them not his, nothing else could. That labour put a distinction between them and common; that added something to them more than nature, the common mother of all, had done, and so they became his private right. And will any one say he had no right to those acorns or apples he thus appropriated, because he had not the consent of all mankind to make them his? Was it a robbery thus to assume to himself what belonged to all in common? If such a consent as that was necessary, man had starved, notwithstanding the plenty God had given him. We see in commons which remain so by compact that 'tis the taking any part of what is common and removing it out of the state nature leaves it in, which begins the property; without which the common is of no use. And the taking of this or that part does not depend on the express consent of all the commoners. Thus the grass my horse has bit, the turfs my servant has cut, and the ore I have dug in any place where I have a right to them in common with others, become my property without the assignation or consent of anybody. The labour that was mine removing them out of that common state they were in, hath fixed my property in them.

29. By making an explicit consent of every commoner necessary to any one's appropriating to himself any part of what is given in common, children or servants could not cut the meat which their father or master had provided for them in common without assigning to every one his peculiar part. Though the water running in the fountain be every one's, yet who can doubt but that in the pitcher is his only who drew it out? His labour hath taken it out of the hands of nature, where it was common, and belonged equally to all her children, and hath thereby appropriated it to himself.

30. Thus this law of reason makes the deer that Indian's who hath

killed it; 'tis allowed to be his goods who hath bestowed his labour upon it, though before it was the common right of every one. And amongst those who are counted the civilized part of mankind, who have made and multiplied positive laws to determine property, this original law of nature, for the beginning of property in what was before common, still takes place; and by virtue thereof, what fish any one catches in the ocean, that great and still remaining common of mankind, or what ambergris any one takes up here, is, by the labour that removes it out of that common state nature left it in, made his property who takes that pains about it. And even amongst us, the hare that any one is hunting is thought his who pursues her during the chase. For being a beast that is still looked upon as common, and no man's private possession, whoever has employed so much labour about any of that kind as to find and pursue her has thereby removed her from the state of nature wherein she was common, and hath begun a property.

31. It will perhaps be objected to this, that if gathering the acorns, or other fruits of the earth, etc., makes a right to them, then any one may engross as much as he will. To which I answer, Not so. The same law of nature, that does by this means give us property, does also bound that property too. "God has given us all things richly" (1 Tim. vi. 12), is the voice of reason confirmed by inspiration. But how far has he given it us? To enjoy. As much as any one can make use of to any advantage of life before it spoils, so much he may by his labour fix a property in; whatever is beyond this is more than his share, and belongs to others. Nothing was made by God for man to spoil or destroy. And thus considering the plenty of natural provisions there was a long time in the world, and the few spenders, and to how small a part of that provision the industry of one man could extend itself, and engross it to the prejudice of others—especially keeping within the bounds, set by reason, of what might serve for his use—there could be then little room for quarrels or contentions about property so established.

32. But the chief matter of property being now not the fruits of the earth, and the beasts that subsist on it, but the earth itself, as that which takes in and carries with it all the rest, I think it is plain that property in that, too, is acquired as the former. As much land as a man tills, plants, improves, cultivates, and can use the product of, so much is his property. He by his labour does as it were enclose it from the common. Nor will it invalidate his right to say, everybody else has an equal title to it; and therefore he cannot appropriate, he cannot enclose, without the consent of all his fellow-commoners, all mankind. God, when he gave the world in common to all mankind, commanded man also to labour, and the penury of his condition required it of him. God and his reason commanded him to subdue the earth, *i.e.*, improve it for the

benefit of life, and therein lay out something upon it that was his own, his labour. He that, in obedience to this command of God, subdued, tilled, and sowed any part of it, thereby annexed to it something that was his property, which another had no title to, nor could without injury take from him.

33. Nor was this appropriation of any parcel of land, by improving it, any prejudice to any other man, since there was still enough and as good left; and more than the yet unprovided could use. So that in effect there was never the less left for others because of his enclosure for himself. For he that leaves as much as another can make use of, does as good as take nothing at all. Nobody could think himself injured by the drinking of another man, though he took a good draught, who had a whole river of the same water left him to quench his thirst; and the case of land and water, where there is enough of both, is perfectly the same.

34. God gave the world to men in common; but since he gave it them for their benefit, and the greatest conveniencies of life they were capable to draw from it, it cannot be supposed he meant it should always remain common and uncultivated. He gave it to the use of the industrious and rational (and labour was to be his title to it), not to the fancy or covetousness of the quarrelsome and contentious. He that had as good left for his improvement as was already taken up, needed not complain, ought not to meddle with what was already improved by another's labour; if he did, 'tis plain he desired the benefit of another's pains, which he had no right to, and not the ground which God had given him in common with others to labour on, and whereof there was as good left as that already possessed, and more than he knew what to do with, or his industry could reach to.

35. 'Tis true, in land that is common in England, or any other country where there is plenty of people under government, who have money and commerce, no one can enclose or appropriate any part without the consent of all his fellow-commoners: because this is left common by compact, *i.e.*, by the law of the land, which is not to be violated. And though it be common in respect of some men, it is not so to all mankind; but is the joint property of this country, or this parish. Besides, the remainder, after such enclosure, would not be as good to the rest of the commoners as the whole was, when they could all make use of the whole; whereas in the beginning and first peopling of the great common of the world it was quite otherwise. The law man was under was rather for appropriating. God commanded, and his wants forced him, to labour. That was his property, which could not be taken from him wherever he had fixed it. And hence subduing or cultivating the earth, and having dominion, we see are joined together. The one

gave title to the other. So that God, by commanding to subdue, gave authority so far to appropriate. And the condition of human life, which requires labour and materials to work on, necessarily introduces private possessions.

36. The measure of property nature has well set by the extent of men's labour and the conveniencies of life. No man's labour could subdue or appropriate all; nor could his enjoyment consume more than a small part; so that it was impossible for any man, this way, to intrench upon the right of another, or acquire to himself a property to the prejudice of his neighbour, who would still have room for as good and as large a possession (after the other had taken out his) as before it was appropriated. This[1] measure did confine every man's possession to a very moderate proportion, and such as he might appropriate to himself without injury to anybody, in the first ages of the world, when men were more in danger to be lost by wandering from their company in the then vast wilderness of the earth than to be straitened for want of room to plant in. And the same measure may be allowed still without prejudice to anybody, as full as the world seems. For supposing a man or family in the state they were at first peopling of the world by the children of Adam or Noah; let him plant in some inland vacant places of America, we shall find that the possessions he could make himself, upon the measures we have given, would not be very large, nor, even to this day, prejudice the rest of mankind, or give them reason to complain or think themselves injured by this man's encroachment, though the race of men have now spread themselves to all the corners of the world, and do infinitely exceed the small number that was at the beginning. Nay, the extent of ground is of so little value without labour, that I have heard it affirmed that in Spain itself a man may be permitted to plough, sow, and reap, without being disturbed, upon land he has no other title to but only his making use of it. But, on the contrary, the inhabitants think themselves beholden to him who by his industry on neglected and consequently waste land has increased the stock of corn which they wanted. But be this as it will, which I lay no stress on, this I dare boldly affirm—that the same rule of propriety, *viz.*, that every man should have as much as he could make use of, would hold still in the world without straitening anybody, since there is land enough in the world to suffice double the inhabitants, had not the invention of money, and the tacit agreement of men to put a value on it, introduced (by consent) larger possessions and a right to them; which how it has done I shall by and by shew more at large.

---

1. This: 6th edition. Earlier editions read: "Which." Collected edition omits the word altogether, and reads: ". . . appropriated. Measure did confine . . ."

37. This is certain, that in the beginning, before the desire of having more than man needed had altered the intrinsic value of things, which depends only on their usefulness to the life of man; or had agreed that a little piece of yellow metal which would keep without wasting or decay should be worth a great piece of flesh or a whole heap of corn, though men had a right to appropriate by their labour, each one to himself, as much of the things of nature as he could use, yet this could not be much, nor to the prejudice of others, where the same plenty was still left to those who would use the same industry. To which let me add[2], that he who appropriates land to himself by his labour does not lessen but increase the common stock of mankind. For the provisions serving to the support of human life produced by one acre of enclosed and cultivated land are (to speak much within compass) ten times more than those which are yielded by an acre of land of an equal richness lying waste in common. And therefore he that encloses land, and has a greater plenty of the conveniencies of life from ten acres than he could have from an hundred left to nature, may truly be said to give ninety acres to mankind: for his labour now supplies him with provisions out of ten acres, which were but the product of an hundred lying in common. I have here rated the improved land very low, in making its product but as ten to one, when it is much nearer an hundred to one. For I ask, whether in the wild woods and uncultivated waste of America, left to nature without any improvement, tillage, or husbandry, a thousand acres yield the needy and wretched inhabitants as many conveniencies of life as ten acres of equally fertile land do in Devonshire, where they are well cultivated?[2]

Before the appropriation of land, he who gathered as much of the wild fruit, killed, caught, or tamed as many of the beasts as he could; he that so employed his pains about any of the spontaneous products of nature as any way to alter them from the state which nature put them in, by placing any of his labour on them, did thereby acquire a propriety in them. But if they perished in his possession without their due use: if the fruits rotted, or the venison putrefied before he could spend it, he offended against the common law of nature, and was liable to be punished; he invaded his neighbour's share, for he had no right farther than his use called for any of them and they might serve to afford him conveniencies of life.

38. The same measures governed the possession of land too. Whatsoever he tilled and reaped, laid up, and made use of before it spoiled, that was his peculiar right; whatsoever he enclosed and could

---

2. The words "To which let me add . . . well cultivated" were added in the collected edition.

feed and make use of, the cattle and product was also his. But if either the grass of his enclosure rotted on the ground, or the fruit of his planting perished without gathering and laying up, this part of the earth, notwithstanding his enclosure, was still to be looked on as waste, and might be the possession of any other. Thus, at the beginning, Cain might take as much ground as he could till and make it his own land, and yet leave enough for Abel's sheep to feed on; a few acres would serve for both their possessions. But as families increased, and industry enlarged their stocks, their possessions enlarged with the need of them; but yet it was commonly without any fixed property in the ground they made use of, till they incorporated, settled themselves together, and built cities; and then, by consent, they came in time to set out the bounds of their distinct territories, and agree on limits between them and their neighbours, and, by laws within themselves, settled the properties of those of the same society. For we see that in that part of the world which was first inhabited, and therefore like to be the best peopled, even as low down as Abraham's time they wandered with their flocks and their herds, which were their substance, freely up and down; and this Abraham did in a country where he was a stranger: whence it is plain that at least a great part of the land lay in common; that the inhabitants valued it not, nor claimed property in any more than they made use of. But when there was not room enough in the same place for their herds to feed together, they by consent, as Abraham and Lot did (Gen. xiii. 5), separated and enlarged their pasture where it best liked them. And for the same reason Esau went from his father and his brother, and planted in Mount Seir (Gen. xxxvi. 6).

39. And thus, without supposing any private dominion and property in Adam over all the world, exclusive of all other men, which can no way be proved, nor any one's property be made out from it; but supposing the world given as it was to the children of men in common, we see how labour could make men distinct titles to several parcels of it for their private uses, wherein there could be no doubt of right, no room for quarrel.

40. Nor is it so strange, as perhaps before consideration it may appear, that the property of labour should be able to overbalance the community of land. For 'tis labour indeed that puts the difference of value on everything; and let any one consider what the difference is between an acre of land planted with tobacco or sugar, sown with wheat or barley, and an acre of the same land lying in common without any husbandry upon it, and he will find that the improvement of labour makes the far greater part of the value. I think it will be but a very modest computation to say that of the products of the earth useful to the life of man nine-tenths are the effects of labour; nay, if we will rightly esti-

mate things as they come to our use, and cast up the several expenses about them—what in them is purely owing to nature, and what to labour—we shall find that in most of them ninety-nine hundredths are wholly to be put on the account of labour.

41. There cannot be a clearer demonstration of anything than several nations of the Americans are of this, who are rich in land and poor in all the comforts of life; whom nature having furnished as liberally as any other people with the materials of plenty—*i.e.*, a fruitful soil, apt to produce in abundance what might serve for food, raiment, and delight—yet, for want of improving it by labour, have not one-hundredth part of the conveniencies we enjoy. And a king of a large and fruitful territory there, feeds, lodges, and is clad worse than a day-labourer in England.

42. To make this a little clearer, let us but trace some of the ordinary provisions of life through their several progresses before they come to our use, and see how much they receive of their value from human industry. Bread, wine, and cloth are things of daily use and great plenty; yet, notwithstanding, acorns, water, and leaves or skins must be our bread, drink, and clothing, did not labour furnish us with these more useful commodities. For whatever bread is more worth than acorns, wine than water, and cloth or silk than leaves, skins, or moss, that is wholly owing to labour and industry; the one of these being the food and raiment which unassisted nature furnishes us with; the other, provisions which our industry and pains prepare for us; which how much they exceed the other in value when any one hath computed, he will then see how much labour makes the far greatest part of the value of things we enjoy in this world. And the ground which produces the materials is scarce to be reckoned in as any, or at most but a very small, part of it; so little that even amongst us land that is left wholly to nature, that hath no improvement of pasturage, tillage, or planting, is called, as indeed it is, waste, and we shall find the benefit of it amount to little more than nothing.

This shows how much numbers of men are to be preferred to largeness of dominions; and that the increase of lands[3] and the right employing of them is the great art of government: and that prince, who shall be so wise and godlike as by established laws of liberty to secure

---

3. It might appear from the context that this is an error for *hands*, and the word is so corrected in a MS. insertion in a copy of the 2nd edition in the Bodleian Library. But the word is printed *lands* in the collected and 6th editions, and it is clearly written so in the MS. insertion in Locke's handwriting in the copy of the 3rd edition in Christ's College Library, on which the 6th edition was based. What Locke meant, presumably, was not the extension of territory, but the proper use of it, by improvement and cultivation, so as to increase its productivity.

protection and encouragement to the honest industry of mankind, against the oppression of power and narrowness of party, will quickly be too hard for his neighbours: but this by the by.

To return to the argument in hand.[4]

43. An acre of land that bears here twenty bushels of wheat, and another in America which, with the same husbandry, would do the like, are without doubt of the same natural intrinsic value; but yet the benefit mankind receives from the one in a year is worth £5, and from the other possibly not worth a penny, if all the profit an Indian received from it were to be valued and sold here; at least, I may truly say, not one-thousandth. 'Tis labour, then, which puts the greatest part of value upon land, without which it would scarcely be worth anything; 'tis to that we owe the greatest part of all its useful products, for all that the straw, bran, bread of that acre of wheat is more worth than the product of an acre of as good land which lies waste, is all the effect of labour. For 'tis not barely the ploughman's pains, the reaper's and thresher's toil, and the baker's sweat, is to be counted into the bread we eat; the labour of those who broke the oxen, who digged and wrought the iron and stones, who felled and framed the timber employed about the plough, mill, oven, or any other utensils, which are a vast number, requisite to this corn, from its being seed to be sown[5] to its being made bread, must all be charged on the account of labour, and received as an effect of that. Nature and the earth furnished only the almost worthless materials as in themselves. 'Twould be a strange catalogue of things that industry provided and made use of, about every loaf of bread before it came to our use, if we could trace them—iron, wood, leather, bark, timber, stone, bricks, coals, lime, cloth, dyeing drugs, pitch, tar, masts, ropes, and all the materials made use of in the ship that brought any of the commodities made use of by any of the workmen to any part of the work, all which 'twould be almost impossible, at least too long, to reckon up.

44. From all which it is evident that, though the things of nature are given in common, yet man, by being master of himself and proprietor of his own person and the actions or labour of it, had still in himself the great foundations of property; and that which made up the great part of what he applied to the support or comfort of his being, when invention and arts had improved the conveniencies of life, was perfectly his own, and did not belong in common to others.

45. Thus labour, in the beginning, gave a right of property, wherever

---

4. The words "This shows how much . . . argument in hand" were added in the collected edition.

5. Collected edition. Earlier editions read: "from its sowing."

any one was pleased to employ it upon what was common, which remained a long while the far greater part, and is yet more than mankind makes use of. Men at first, for the most part, contented themselves with what unassisted nature offered to their necessities; and though afterwards, in some parts of the world (where the increase of people and stock, with the use of money, had made land scarce, and so of some value), the several communities settled the bounds of their distinct territories, and, by laws within themselves, regulated the properties of the private men of their society, and so, by compact and agreement, settled the property which labour and industry began—and the leagues that have been made between several states and kingdoms, either expressly or tacitly disowning all claim and right to the land in the other's possession, have, by common consent, given up their pretences to their natural common right, which originally they had to those countries; and so have, by positive agreement, settled a property amongst themselves in distinct parts and parcels of the earth[6]—yet there are still great tracts of ground to be found which (the inhabitants thereof not having joined with the rest of mankind in the consent of the use of their common money) lie waste, and are more than the people who dwell on it do or can make use of, and so still lie in common; though this can scarce happen amongst that part of mankind that have consented to the use of money.

46. The greatest part of things really useful to the life of man, and such as the necessity of subsisting made the first commoners of the world look after, as it doth the Americans now, are generally things of short duration, such as, if they are not consumed by use, will decay and perish of themselves: gold, silver, and diamonds are things that fancy or agreement have put the value on more than real use and the necessary support of life. Now, of those good things which nature hath provided in common, every one had a right (as hath been said) to as much as he could use, and property[7] in all he could effect with his labour; all that his industry could extend to, to alter from the state nature had put it in, was his. He that gathered a hundred bushels of acorns or apples had thereby a property in them; they were his goods as soon as gathered. He was only to look that he used them before they spoiled, else he took more than his share, and robbed others; and, indeed, it was a foolish thing, as well as dishonest, to hoard up more than he could make use of. If he gave away a part to anybody else, so that it perished not uselessly in his possession, these he also made use of; and if he also

---

6. Collected edition. Earlier editions read: "parts of the world."

7. Collected edition. Earlier editions read: "hath a right, . . . and had a property in all . . ."

bartered away plums that would have rotted in a week, for nuts that would last good for his eating a whole year, he did no injury; he wasted not the common stock, destroyed no part of the portion of goods that belonged to others, so long as nothing perished uselessly in his hands. Again, if he would give his nuts for a piece of metal, pleased with its colour; or exchange his sheep for shells, or wool for a sparkling pebble or a diamond, and keep those by him all his life, he invaded not the right of others; he might heap up as much of these durable things as he pleased, the exceeding of the bounds of his just property not lying in the largeness of his possession, but the perishing of anything uselessly in it.

47. And thus came in the use of money—some lasting thing that men might keep without spoiling, and that, by mutual consent, men would take in exchange for the truly useful but perishable supports of life.

48. And as different degrees of industry were apt to give men possessions in different proportions, so this invention of money gave them the opportunity to continue and enlarge them; for supposing an island, separate from all possible commerce with the rest of the world, wherein there were but an hundred families—but there were sheep, horses, and cows, with other useful animals, wholesome fruits, and land enough for corn for a hundred thousand times as many, but nothing in the island, either because of its commonness or perishableness, fit to supply the place of money—what reason could any one have there to enlarge his possessions beyond the use of his family and a plentiful supply to its consumption, either in what their own industry produced, or they could barter for like perishable useful commodities with others? Where there is not something both lasting and scarce, and so valuable to be hoarded up, there men will not be apt to enlarge their possessions of land, were it never so rich, never so free for them to take; for I ask, what would a man value ten thousand or an hundred thousand acres of excellent land, ready cultivated, and well stocked too with cattle, in the middle of the inland parts of America, where he had no hopes of commerce with other parts of the world, to draw money to him by the sale of the product? It would not be worth the enclosing, and we should see him give up again to the wild common of nature whatever was more than would supply the conveniencies of life to be had there for him and his family.

49. Thus in the beginning all the world was America, and more so than that is now, for no such thing as money was anywhere known. Find out something that hath the use and value of money amongst his neighbours, you shall see the same man will begin presently to enlarge his possessions.

50. But since gold and silver, being little useful to the life of man in proportion to food, raiment, and carriage, has its value only from the consent of men, whereof labour yet makes, in great part, the measure, it is plain that men[8] have agreed to a disproportionate and unequal possession of the earth; they[9] having, by a tacit and voluntary consent, found out a way how a man may fairly possess more land than he himself can use the product of, by receiving in exchange for the overplus, gold and silver, which may be hoarded up without injury to any one; these metals not spoiling or decaying in the hands of the possessor. This partage of things in an inequality[10] of private possessions men have made practicable, out of the bounds of society, and without compact, only by putting a value on gold and silver, and tacitly agreeing in the use of money. For in governments the laws regulate the right of property, and the possession of land is determined by positive constitutions.[9]

51. And thus, I think, it is very easy to conceive without any difficulty how labour could at first begin a title of property in the common things of nature, and how the spending it upon our uses bounded it; so that there could then be no reason of quarrelling about title, nor any doubt about the largeness of possession it gave. Right and conveniency went together; for as a man had a right to all he could employ his labour upon, so he had no temptation to labour for more than he could make use of. This left no room for controversy about the title, nor for encroachment on the right of others; what portion a man carved to himself was easily seen, and it was useless, as well as dishonest, to carve himself too much, or take more than he needed.

Chapter VI

Of Paternal Power

52. It may perhaps be censured as an impertinent criticism in a discourse of this nature to find fault with words and names that have ob-

---

8. Collected edition. Earlier editions read: ". . . plain that the consent of men have agreed . . ."

9. Collected edition. Earlier editions read: "I mean out of the bounds of society and compact; for in governments the laws regulate it; they having, by consent, found out and agreed in a way how a man may rightfully and without injury possess more than he himself can make use of by receiving gold and silver, which may continue long in a man's possession, without decaying for the overplus, and agreeing those metals should have a value."

10. Corrected in 6th edition. Collected edition reads: "equality."

tained in the world, and yet possibly it may not be amiss to offer new ones when the old are apt to lead men into mistakes, as this of paternal power probably has done, which seems so to place the power of parents over their children wholly in the father, as if the mother had no share in it; whereas, if we consult reason or revelation, we shall find she hath an equal title. This may give one reason to ask whether this might not be more properly called parental power? For whatever obligation nature and the right of generation lays on children, it must certainly bind them equal to both the concurrent causes of it. And accordingly we see the positive law of God everywhere joins them together without distinction when it commands the obedience of children. "Honour thy father and thy mother" (Exod. xx. 12); "Whosoever curseth his father or his mother" (Lev. xx. 9); "Ye shall fear every man his mother and his father" (Lev. xix. 3); "Children, obey your parents," etc. (Eph. vi. 1), is the style of the Old and New Testament.

53. Had but this one thing been well considered, without looking any deeper into the matter, it might, perhaps, have kept men from running into those gross mistakes they have made about this power of parents; which, however it might without any great harshness bear the name of absolute dominion and regal authority when, under the title of paternal power, it seemed appropriated to the father, would yet have sounded but oddly, and in the very name shewn the absurdity, if this supposed absolute power over children had been called parental, and thereby have discovered that it belonged to the mother too. For it will but very ill serve the turn of those men who contend so much for the absolute power and authority of the fatherhood, as they call it, that the mother should have any share in it. And it would have but ill supported the monarchy they contend for, when by the very name it appeared that the fundamental authority from whence they would derive their government of a single person only, was not placed in one, but two persons jointly. But to let this of names pass.

54. Though I have said above (Chapter II) that all men by nature are equal, I cannot be supposed to understand all sorts of equality. Age or virtue may give men a just precedency. Excellency of parts and merit may place others above the common level. Birth may subject some, and alliance or benefits others, to pay an observance to those to whom nature, gratitude, or other respects may have made it due. And yet all this consists with the equality which all men are in, in respect of jurisdiction or dominion one over another; which was the equality I there spoke of as proper to the business in hand, being that equal right that every man hath to his natural freedom, without being subjected to the will or authority of any other man.

55. Children, I confess, are not born in this full state of equality,

though they are born to it. Their parents have a sort of rule and jurisdiction over them when they come into the world, and for some time
after, but 'tis but a temporary one. The bonds of this subjection are like
the swaddling clothes they are wrapped up in and supported by in the
weakness of their infancy. Age and reason, as they grow up, loosen
them, till at length they drop quite off, and leave a man at his own free
disposal.

56. Adam was created a perfect man, his body and mind in full possession of their strength and reason, and so was capable, from the first
instant of his being, to provide for his own support and preservation,
and govern his actions according to the dictates of the law of reason
which God had implanted in him. From him the world is peopled with
his descendants, who are all born infants, weak and helpless, without
knowledge or understanding. But to supply the defects of this imperfect
state till the improvement of growth and age hath removed them,
Adam and Eve, and after them all parents, were by the law of nature
under an obligation to preserve, nourish, and educate the children they
had begotten; not as their own workmanship, but the workmanship of
their own Maker, the Almighty to whom they were to be accountable
for them.

57. The law that was to govern Adam was the same that was to govern all his posterity, the law of reason. But his offspring having another
way of entrance into the world, different from him, by a natural birth,
that produced them ignorant and without the use of reason, they were
not presently under that law. For nobody can be under a law which is
not promulgated to him; and this law being promulgated or made
known by reason only, he that is not come to the use of his reason cannot be said to be under this law; and Adam's children being not
presently as soon as born under this law of reason, were not presently
free. For law in its true notion is not so much the limitation as the direction of a free and intelligent agent to his proper interest, and prescribes no farther than is for the general good of those under that law;
could they be happier without it, the law as an useless thing would of
itself vanish; and that ill deserves the name of confinement which
hedges us in only from bogs and precipices. So that, however it may be
mistaken, the end of law is, not to abolish or restrain, but to preserve
and enlarge freedom. For in all the states of created beings capable of
laws, where there is no law there is no freedom. For liberty is to be free
from restraint and violence from others; which cannot be where there
is no law: but freedom[1] is not, as we are told, a liberty for every man to
do what he lists (for who could be free when every other man's humour

---

1. Collected edition. Earlier editions read: ". . . no law: and is not . . ."

might domineer over him?), but a liberty to dispose, and order as he lists, his person, actions, possessions, and his whole property, within the allowance of those laws under which he is, and therein not to be subject to the arbitrary will of another, but freely follow his own.

58. The power, then, that parents have over their children arises from that duty which is incumbent on them, to take care of their offspring during the imperfect state of childhood. To inform the mind, and govern the actions of their yet ignorant nonage, till reason shall take its place and ease them of that trouble, is what the children want, and the parents are bound to. For God, having given man an understanding to direct his actions, has allowed him a freedom of will and liberty of acting as properly belonging thereunto, within the bounds of that law he is under. But whilst he is in an estate wherein he has not understanding of his own to direct his will, he is not to have any will of his own to follow. He that understands for him must will for him too; he must prescribe to his will, and regulate his actions; but when he comes to the estate that made his father a freeman, the son is a freeman too.

59. This holds in all the laws a man is under, whether natural or civil. Is a man under the law of nature? What made him free of that law? What gave him a free disposing of his property according to his own will within the compass of that law? I answer, A state of maturity,[2] wherein he might be supposed capable to know that law, that so he might keep his actions within the bounds of it. When he has acquired that state, he is presumed to know how far that law is to be his guide, and how far he may make use of his freedom, and so comes to have it; till then somebody else must guide him, who is presumed to know how far the law allows a liberty. If such a state of reason, such an age of discretion made him free, the same shall make his son free too. Is a man under the law of England? What made him free of that law? That is, to have the liberty to dispose of his actions and possessions according to his own will, within the permission of that law? A capacity of knowing that law; which is supposed by that law at the age of one and twenty years,[3] and in some cases sooner. If this made the father free, it shall make the son free too. Till then we see the law allows the son to have no will, but he is to be guided by the will of his father or guardian, who is to understand for him. And if the father die, and fail to substitute a deputy in his trust; if he hath not provided a tutor to govern his son during his minority, during his want of understanding, the law takes care to do it. Some other must govern him, and be a will to him, till he hath attained to a state of

---

2. The words "of maturity" were added in the 2nd edition. The 1st edition reads: "an estate wherein he . . ."

3. Collected edition. Earlier editions read: "the age of twenty-one."

freedom, and his understanding be fit to take the government of his will. But after that the father and son are equally free, as much as tutor and pupil after nonage; equally subjects of the same law together, without any dominion left in the father over the life, liberty, or estate of his son, whether they be only in the state and under the law of nature, or under the positive laws of an established government.

60. But if, through defects that may happen out of the ordinary course of nature, any one comes not to such a degree of reason wherein he might be supposed capable of knowing the law, and so living within the rules of it, he is never capable of being a free man, he is never let loose to the disposure of his own will (because he knows no bounds to it, has not understanding, its proper guide) but is continued under the tuition and government of others all the time his own understanding is incapable of that charge. And so lunatics and idiots are never set free from the government of their parents; "children who are not as yet come unto those years whereat they may have; and innocents which are excluded by a natural defect from ever having; thirdly, madmen, which for the present cannot possibly have the use of right reason to guide themselves, have for their guide the reason that guideth other men which are tutors over them, to seek and procure their good for them," says Hooker, Eccl. Pol., lib. i, sect. 7. All which seems no more than that duty which God and nature has laid on man, as well as other creatures, to preserve their offspring till they can be able to shift for themselves, and will scarce amount to an instance or proof of parents' regal authority.

61. Thus we are born free, as we are born rational; not that we have actually the exercise of either: age that brings one, brings with it the other too. And thus we see how natural freedom and subjection to parents may consist together, and are both founded on the same principle. A child is free by his father's title, by his father's understanding, which is to govern him till he hath it of his own. The freedom of a man at years of discretion, and the subjection of a child to his parents whilst yet short of that age, are so consistent, and so distinguishable, that the most blinded contenders for monarchy by right of fatherhood cannot miss this difference[4]; the most obstinate cannot but allow their consistency.[5] For were their doctrine all true, were the right heir of Adam now known, and by that title settled a monarch in his throne, invested with all the absolute unlimited power Sir Robert Filmer talks of; if he should die as soon as his heir were born, must not the child, notwithstanding he were never so free, never so much sovereign, be in subjection to his

---

4. 2nd edition. 1st edition reads: ". . . miss of it."
5. 2nd edition. 1st edition reads: ". . . allow of it."

mother and nurse, to tutors and governors, till age and education brought him reason and ability to govern himself and others? The necessities of his life, the health of his body, and the information of his mind would require him to be directed by the will of others and not his own; and yet will any one think that this restraint and subjection were inconsistent with, or spoiled him of that liberty or sovereignty he had a right to, or gave away his empire to those who had the government of his nonage? This government over him only prepared him the better and sooner for it. If anybody should ask me when my son is of age to be free, I shall answer, Just when his monarch is of age to govern. "But at what time," says the judicious Hooker, Eccl. Pol., lib. i, sect. 6, "a man may be said to have attained so far forth the use of reason as sufficeth to make him capable of those laws whereby he is then bound to guide his actions, this is a great deal more easy for sense to discern than for any one by skill and learning to determine."

62. Commonwealths themselves take notice of and allow that there is a time when men are to begin to act like free men, and therefore till that time require not oaths of fealty or allegiance, or other public owning of, or submission to, the government of their countries.

63. The freedom, then, of man, and liberty of acting according to his own will, is grounded on his having reason, which is able to instruct him in that law he is to govern himself by, and make him know how far he is left to the freedom of his own will. To turn him loose to an unrestrained liberty before he has reason to guide him is not the allowing him the privilege of his nature to be free, but to thrust him out amongst brutes, and abandon him to a state as wretched, and as much beneath that of a man, as theirs. This is that which puts the authority into the parents' hands to govern the minority of their children. God hath made it their business to employ this care on their offspring, and hath placed in them suitable inclinations of tenderness and concern to temper this power, to apply it, as his wisdom designed it, to the children's good, as long as they should need to be under it.

64. But what reason can hence advance this care of the parents due to their offspring into an absolute arbitrary dominion of the father? whose power reaches no farther than by such a discipline as he finds most effectual to give such strength and health to their bodies, such vigour and rectitude to their minds, as may best fit his children to be most useful to themselves and others; and, if it be necessary to this condition, to make them work, when they are able, for their own subsistence. But in this power the mother, too, has her share with the father.

65. Nay, this power so little belongs to the father by any peculiar right of nature, but only as he is guardian of his children, that when he quits his care of them he loses his power over them, which goes along

with their nourishment and education, to which it is inseparably annexed, and it belongs as much to the foster-father of an exposed child as the natural father of another; so little power does the bare act of begetting give a man over his issue, if all his care ends there, and this be all the title he hath to the name and authority of a father. And what will become of this paternal power in that part of the world where one woman hath more than one husband at a time? Or in those parts of America where, when the husband and wife part, which happens frequently, the children are all left to the mother, follow her, and are wholly under her care and provision? If the father die whilst the children are young, do they not naturally everywhere owe the same obedience to their mother during their minority as to their father were he alive? And will any one say that the mother hath a legislative power over her children? That she can make standing rules, which shall be of perpetual obligation, by which they ought to regulate all the concerns of their property, and bound their liberty all the course of their lives? Or can she[6] enforce the observation of them with capital punishments? For this is the proper power of the magistrate, of which the father hath not so much as the shadow. His command over his children is but temporary, and reaches not their life or property; it is but a help to the weakness and imperfection of their nonage, a discipline necessary to their education; and though a father may dispose of his own possessions as he pleases when his children are out of danger of perishing for want, yet his power extends not to the lives or goods, which either their own industry or another's bounty has made theirs; nor to their liberty neither, when they are once arrived to the enfranchisement of the years of discretion. The father's empire then ceases, and he can from thenceforwards no more dispose of the liberty of his son than that of any other man; and it must be far from an absolute or perpetual jurisdiction, from which a man may withdraw himself, having licence from divine authority to leave father and mother and cleave to his wife.

66. But though there be a time when a child comes to be as free from subjection to the will and command of his father, as the father[7] himself is free from subjection to the will of anybody else, and they are each[8] under no other restraint but that which is common to them both, whether it be the law of nature or municipal law of their country, yet this freedom exempts not a son from that honour which he ought, by the law of God and nature, to pay his parents. God having made the parents in-

6. Altered in list of *errata* in 2nd edition. 1st edition reads: ". . . of their lives, and inforce . . ."

7. Altered in collected edition. Earlier editions read: ". . . his father, as he himself is free . . ."

8. Altered in *errata* list in 3rd edition. Earlier editions read: "both."

struments in his great design of continuing the race of mankind, and the occasions of life to their children, as he hath laid on them an obligation to nourish, preserve, and bring up their offspring, so he has laid on the children a perpetual obligation of honouring their parents, which containing in it an inward esteem and reverence to be shewn by all outward expressions, ties up the child from anything that may ever injure or affront, disturb, or endanger the happiness or life of those from whom he received his; and engages him in all actions of defence, relief, assistance, and comfort of those by whose means he entered into being, and has been made capable of any enjoyments of life. From this obligation no state, no freedom, can absolve children. But this is very far from giving parents a power of command over their children, or an authority to make laws and dispose as they please of their lives or liberties. 'Tis one thing to owe honour, respect, gratitude, and assistance; another to require an absolute obedience and submission. The honour due to parents, a monarch in his throne owes his mother, and yet this lessens not his authority, nor subjects him to her government.

67. The subjection of a minor places in the father a temporary government, which terminates with the minority of the child; and the honour due from a child places in the parents a perpetual right to respect, reverence, support, and compliance too, more or less, as the father's care, cost, and kindness in his education has been more or less. This ends not with minority, but holds in all parts and conditions of a man's life. The want of distinguishing these two powers, *viz.*, that[9] which the father hath in the right of tuition during minority, and the right of honour all his life, may perhaps have caused a great part of the mistakes about this matter. For, to speak properly of them, the first of these is rather the privilege of children, and duty of parents, than any prerogative of paternal power. The nourishment and education of their children is a charge so incumbent on parents for their children's good that nothing can absolve them from taking care of it. And though the power of commanding and chastising them go along with it, yet God hath woven into the principles of human nature such a tenderness for their offspring that there is little fear that parents should use their power with too much rigour; the excess is seldom on the severe side, the strong bias of nature drawing the other way. And therefore God Almighty, when he would express his gentle dealing with the Israelites, he tells them that though he chastened them, he chastened them as a man chastens his son (Deut. viii. 5)—*i.e.*, with tenderness and affection—and kept them under no severer discipline than what was absolutely best for them, and had been less kindness to have slackened. This is that power to which

---

9. Added in collected edition. Earlier editions read: "... powers which the father ..."

children are commanded obedience, that the pains and care of their parents may not be increased or ill rewarded.

68. On the other side, honour and support, all that which gratitude requires to return for the benefits received by and from them, is the indispensable duty of the child, and the proper privilege of the parents. This is intended for the parents' advantage, as the other is for the child's, though education, the parents' duty, seems to have most power, because the ignorance and infirmities of childhood stand in need of restraint and correction, which is a visible exercise of rule, and a kind of dominion. And that duty which is comprehended in the word honour requires less obedience, though the obligation be stronger on grown than younger children. For who can think the command, "Children, obey your parents," requires in a man that has children of his own the same submission to his father as it does in his yet young children to him, and that by this precept he were bound to obey all his father's commands if, out of a conceit of authority, he should have the indiscretion to treat him still as a boy?

69. The first part, then, of paternal power, or rather duty, which is education, belongs so to the father that it terminates at a certain season. When the business of education is over, it ceases of itself, and is also alienable before. For a man may put the tuition of his son in other hands; and he that has made his son an apprentice to another has discharged him during that time of a great part of his obedience, both to himself and to his mother. But all the duty of honour, the other part, remains, nevertheless, entire to them; nothing can cancel that. It is so inseparable from them both that the father's authority cannot dispossess the mother of this right, nor can any man discharge his son from honouring her that bore him. But both these are very far from a power to make laws, and enforcing them with penalties that may reach estate, liberty, limbs, and life. The power of commanding ends with nonage; and though after that, honour and respect, support and defence, and whatsoever gratitude can oblige a man to, for the highest benefits he is naturally capable of, be always due from a son to his parents, yet all this puts no sceptre into the father's hand, no sovereign power of commanding. He has no dominion over his son's property or actions, nor any right that his will should prescribe to his son's in all things, however it may become his son in many things not very inconvenient to him and his family to pay a deference to it.

70. A man may owe honour and respect to an ancient or wise man, defence to his child or friend, relief and support to the distressed, and gratitude to a benefactor, to such a degree that all he has, all he can do, cannot sufficiently pay it; but all these give no authority, no right to any one of making laws over him from whom they are owing. And 'tis plain

all this is due not only to the bare title of father, not only because, as has been said, it is owing to the mother, too, but because these obligations to parents, and the degrees of what is required of children, may be varied by the different care and kindness, trouble and expense, which is often employed upon one child more than another.

71. This shows the reason how it comes to pass that parents in societies, where they themselves are subjects, retain a power over their children, and have as much right to their subjection, as those who are in the state of nature. Which could not possibly be if all political power were only paternal, and that in truth they were one and the same thing; for then all paternal power being in the prince, the subject could naturally have none of it. But these two powers, political and paternal, are so perfectly distinct and separate, are built upon so different foundations, and given to so different ends, that every subject that is a father has as much a paternal power over his children as the prince has over his; and every prince that has parents owes them as much filial duty and obedience as the meanest of his subjects do to theirs, and can therefore contain not any part or degree of that kind of dominion which a prince or magistrate has over his subject.

72. Though the obligation on the parents to bring up their children, and the obligation on children to honour their parents, contain all the power on the one hand, and submission on the other, which are proper to this relation, yet there is another power ordinarily in the father, whereby he has a tie on the obedience of his children; which, though it be common to him with other men, yet the occasions of shewing it almost constantly happening to fathers in their private families, and the instances of it elsewhere being rare, and less taken notice of, it passes in the world for a part of paternal jurisdiction. And this is the power men generally have to bestow their estates on those who please them best. The possession of the father being the expectation and inheritance of the children, ordinarily in certain proportions, according to the law and custom of each country, yet it is commonly in the father's power to bestow it with a more sparing or liberal hand, according as the behaviour of this or that child hath comported with his will and humour.

73. This is no small tie on the obedience of children. And there being always annexed to the enjoyment of land a submission to the government of the country of which that land is a part, it has been commonly supposed that a father could oblige his posterity to that government of which he himself was a subject, and that his compact held them; whereas, it being only a necessary condition annexed to the land, and the inheritance of an estate[10] which is under that government,

---

10. Added in collected edition. Earlier editions read: ". . . land, which is under . . ."

reaches only those who will take it on that condition, and so is no natural tie or engagement, but a voluntary submission. For every man's children being by nature as free as himself, or any of his ancestors ever were, may, whilst they are in that freedom, choose what society they will join themselves to, what commonwealth they will put themselves under. But if they will enjoy the inheritance of their ancestors, they must take it on the same terms their ancestors had it, and submit to all the conditions annexed to such a possession. By this power, indeed, fathers oblige their children to obedience to themselves, even when they are past minority, and most commonly, too, subject them to this or that political power. But neither of these by any peculiar right of fatherhood, but by the reward they have in their hands to enforce and recompense such a compliance; and is no more power than what a Frenchman has over an Englishman, who, by the hopes of an estate he will leave him, will certainly have a strong tie on his obedience. And if, when it is left him, he will enjoy it, he must certainly take it upon the conditions annexed to the possession of land in that country where it lies, whether it be France or England.

74. To conclude, then: though the father's power of commanding extends no farther than the minority of his children, and to a degree only fit for the discipline and government of that age; and though that honour and respect, and all that which the Latins called piety, which they indispensably owe to their parents all their lifetime and in all estates, with all that support and defence is due to them, gives the father no power of governing—*i.e.*, making laws and exacting penalties on his children—though by all[11] this he has no dominion over the property or actions of his son, yet it is obvious to conceive how easy it was, in the first ages of the world, and in places still where the thinness of people gives families leave to separate into unpossessed quarters, and they have room to remove or plant themselves in yet vacant habitations, for the father of the family to become the prince of it.* He had been a ruler

---

11. "All" added in collected edition.

*"It is no improbable opinion, therefore, which the arch-philosopher was of, that the chief person in every household was always, as it were, a king; so when numbers of households joined themselves in civil societies together, kings were the first kind of governors among them, which is also, as it seemeth, the reason why the name of fathers continued still in them, who of fathers were made rulers; as also the ancient custom of governors to do as Melchizedec; and being kings, to exercise the office of priests, which fathers did at the first, grew perhaps by the same occasion. Howbeit, this is not the only kind of regiment that has been received in the world. The inconveniencies of one kind have caused sundry other to be devised, so that, in a word, all public regiment of what kind soever, seemeth evidently to have risen from the deliberate advice, consultation, and composition between men, judging it convenient and behoveful, there being no impossibility in nature, considered by itself, but that man might have lived without any public regiment."—Hooker (*Eccl. Pol.*, lib. i, sect. 10).

from the beginning of the infancy of his children: and since[12] without some government it would be hard for them to live together, it was likeliest it should, by the express or tacit consent of the children, when they were grown up, be in the father, where it seemed without any change barely to continue; when indeed nothing more was required to it than the permitting the father to exercise alone in his family that executive power of the law of nature which every free man naturally hath, and by that permission resigning up to him a monarchical power whilst they remained in it. But that this was not by any paternal right, but only by the consent of his children, is evident from hence—that nobody doubts but if a stranger, whom chance or business had brought to his family, had there killed any of his children, or committed any other fact, he might condemn and put him to death, or otherwise have punished him as well as any of his children, which it was impossible he should do by virtue of any paternal authority over one who was not his child, but by virtue of that executive power of the law of nature which, as a man, he had a right to; and he alone could punish him in his family, where the respect of his children had laid by the exercise of such a power to give way to the dignity and authority they were willing should remain in him above the rest of his family.

75. Thus 'twas easy and almost natural for children by a tacit and scarce avoidable[13] consent to make way for the father's authority and government. They had been accustomed in their childhood to follow his direction, and to refer their little differences to him; and when they were men, who fitter to rule them? Their little properties, and less covetousness, seldom afforded greater controversies; and when they should arise, where could they have a fitter umpire than he by whose care they had every one been sustained and brought up, and who had a tenderness for them all? 'Tis no wonder that they made no distinction betwixt minority and full age; nor looked after one-and-twenty or any other age that might make them the free disposers of themselves and fortunes, when they could have no desire to be out of their pupilage. The government they had been under during it, continued still to be more their protection than restraint; and they could nowhere find a greater security to their peace, liberties, and fortunes, than in the rule of a father.

76. Thus the natural fathers of families by an insensible change became the politic monarchs of them too; and as they chanced to live long and leave able and worthy heirs for several successions or otherwise, so they laid the foundations of hereditary or elective kingdoms

---

12. Collected edition. Earlier editions read: "... children, and when they were grown up; since without ..."

13. Scarce avoidable: collected edition. Earlier editions read: "almost natural."

under several constitutions and manners, according as chance, contrivance, or occasions happened to mould them. But if princes have their titles in their fathers' right, and it be a sufficient proof of the natural right of fathers to political authority, because they commonly were those in whose hands we find *de facto* the exercise of government—I say, if this argument be good, it will as strongly prove that all princes— nay, princes only—ought to be priests, since it is as certain that in the beginning the father of the family was priest, as that he was ruler in his own household.

Chapter VII

Of Political or Civil Society

77. God having made man such a creature, that in his own judgment it was not good for him to be alone, put him under strong obligations of necessity, convenience, and inclination to drive him into society, as well as fitted him with understanding and language to continue and enjoy it. The first society was between man and wife, which gave beginning to that between parents and children; to which, in time, that between master and servant came to be added; and though all these might, and commonly did meet together, and make up but one family, wherein the master or mistress of it had some sort of rule proper to a family; each of these, or all together, came short of political society, as we shall see, if we consider the different ends, ties, and bounds of each of these.

78. Conjugal society is made by a voluntary compact between man and woman, and though it consists chiefly in such a communion and right in one another's bodies as is necessary to its chief end, procreation, yet it draws with it mutual support and assistance, and a communion of interests too, as necessary not only to unite their care and affection, but also necessary to their common offspring, who have a right to be nourished and maintained by them till they are able to provide for themselves.

79. For the end of conjunction between male and female being not barely procreation, but the continuation of the species, this conjunction betwixt male and female ought to last, even after procreation, so long as is necessary to the nourishment and support of the young ones, who are to be sustained by those that got them till they are able to shift and provide for themselves. This rule, which the infinite wise Maker hath set to the works of his hands, we find the inferior creatures steadily obey. In those viviparous animals which feed on grass, the conjunction between male and female lasts no longer than the very act of copula-

tion, because the teat of the dam being sufficient to nourish the young till it be able to feed on grass, the male only begets, but concerns not himself for the female or young, to whose sustenance he can contribute nothing. But in beasts of prey the conjunction lasts longer, because the dam not being able well to subsist herself and nourish her numerous offspring by her own prey alone, a more laborious as well as more dangerous way of living than by feeding on grass, the assistance of the male is necessary to the maintenance of their common family, which cannot subsist till they are able to prey for themselves but by the joint care of male and female. The same is to be observed in all birds (except some domestic ones where plenty of food excuses the cock from feeding and taking care of the young brood), whose young needing food in the nest, the cock and hen continue mates till the young are able to use their wing and provide for themselves.

80. And herein I think lies the chief, if not the only, reason why the male and female in mankind are tied to a longer conjunction than other creatures, *viz.*, because the female is capable of conceiving, and *de facto* is commonly with child again, and brings forth, too, a new birth, long before the former is out of a dependency for support on his parents' help, and able to shift for himself, and has all the assistance is due to him from his parents; whereby the father, who is bound to take care for those he hath begot, is under an obligation to continue in conjugal society with the same woman longer than other creatures, whose young being able to subsist of themselves before the time of procreation returns again, the conjugal bond dissolves of itself, and they are at liberty till Hymen at his usual anniversary season summons them again to choose new mates. Wherein one cannot but admire the wisdom of the great Creator, who having given to man foresight, and[1] an ability to lay up for the future as well as to supply the present necessity, hath made it necessary that society of man and wife should be more lasting than of male and female amongst other creatures, that so their industry might be encouraged, and their interest better united to make provision and lay up goods for their common issue, which uncertain mixture or easy and frequent solutions of conjugal society would mightily disturb.

81. But though these are ties upon mankind which make the conjugal bonds more firm and lasting in man than the other species of animals, yet it would give one reason to inquire why this compact, where procreation and education are secured, and inheritance taken care for, may not be made determinable, either by consent, or at a certain time, or upon certain conditions, as well as any other voluntary compacts, there being no necessity in the nature of the thing, nor to the ends of it, that it should

---

1. Collected edition. Earlier editions read: ". . . to man an ability . . ."

always be for life—I mean to such as are under no restraint of any positive law which ordains all such contracts to be perpetual.

82. But the husband and wife, though they have but one common concern, yet having different understandings, will unavoidably sometimes have different wills too; it therefore being necessary that the last determination—*i.e.*, the rule—should be placed somewhere, it naturally falls to the man's share, as the abler and the stronger. But this, reaching but to the things of their common interest and property, leaves the wife in the full and free[2] possession of what by contract is her peculiar right, and at least gives the husband no more power over her life than she has over his. The power of the husband being so far from that of an absolute monarch, that the wife has in many cases a liberty to separate from him, where natural right or their contract allows it, whether that contract be made by themselves in a state of nature, or by the customs or laws of the country they live in; and the children upon such separation fall to the father's or mother's lot, as such contract does determine.

83. For all the ends of marriage being to be obtained under politic government, as well as in the state of nature, the civil magistrate doth not abridge the right or power of either naturally necessary to those ends—*viz.*, procreation and mutual support and assistance whilst they are together—but only decides any controversy that may arise between man and wife about them. If it were otherwise, and that absolute sovereignty and power of life and death naturally belonged to the husband, and were necessary to the society between man and wife, there could be no matrimony in any of those countries where the husband is allowed no such absolute authority. But the ends of matrimony requiring no such power in the husband, the condition of conjugal society put it not in him, it being not at all necessary to that state. Conjugal society could subsist and attain its ends without it; nay, community of goods, and the power over them, mutual assistance and maintenance, and other things belonging to conjugal society, might be varied and regulated by that contract which unites man and wife in that society, as far as may consist with procreation and the bringing up of children till they could shift for themselves[3]; nothing being necessary to any society that is not necessary to the ends for which it is made.

---

2. "Free" in collected edition. "True" in earlier editions, but marked as an *erratum* in the 3rd edition.

3. Altered in 2nd edition. 1st edition reads: ". . . power in the husband, it was not at all necessary to it: the condition of conjugal society put it not in him, but whatsoever might consist with procreation and support of the children till they could shift for themselves: mutual assistance, comfort, and maintenance might be varied and regulated by that contract which first united them in that society; nothing being necessary . . ."

84. The society betwixt parents and children, and the distinct rights and powers belonging respectively to them, I have treated of so largely in the foregoing chapter that I shall not here need to say anything of it; and I think it is plain that it is far different from a politic society.

85. Master and servant are names as old as history, but given to those of far different condition; for a freeman makes himself a servant to another by selling him for a certain time the service he undertakes to do in exchange for wages he is to receive; and though this commonly puts him into the family of his master, and under the ordinary discipline thereof, yet it gives the master but a temporary power over him, and no greater than what is contained in the contract between them. But there is another sort of servants, which by a peculiar name we call slaves, who, being captives taken in a just war, are by the right of nature subjected to the absolute dominion and arbitrary power of their masters. These men having, as I say, forfeited their lives, and with them their liberties, and lost their estates—and being, in the state of slavery, not capable of any property—cannot in that state be considered as any part of civil society, the chief end whereof is the preservation of property.

86. Let us therefore consider a master of a family, with all these subordinate relations of wife, children, servants, and slaves, united under the domestic rule of a family, which, what resemblance soever it may have in its order, offices, and number too, with a little commonwealth, yet is very far from it both in its constitution, power, and end; or, if it must be thought a monarchy, and the paterfamilias the absolute monarch in it, absolute monarchy will have but a very shattered and short power, when 'tis plain, by what has been said before, that the master of the family has a very distinct and differently limited power, both as to time and extent, over those several persons that are in it; for, excepting the slave (and the family is as much a family, and his power as paterfamilias as great, whether there be any slaves in his family or no), he has no legislative power of life and death over any of them, and none, too, but what a mistress of a family may have as well as he. And he certainly can have no absolute power over the whole family, who has but a very limited one over every individual in it. But how a family or any other society of men differ from that, which is properly political society, we shall best see by considering wherein political society itself consists.

87. Man being born, as has been proved, with a title to perfect freedom, and an uncontrolled enjoyment of all the rights and privileges of the law of nature equally with any other man or number of men in the world, hath by nature a power not only to preserve his property—that is, his life, liberty, and estate—against the injuries and attempts of other men, but to judge of and punish the breaches of that law in others as

he is persuaded the offence deserves, even with death itself, in crimes where the heinousness of the fact in his opinion requires it. But because no political society can be nor subsist without having in itself the power to preserve the property, and, in order thereunto, punish the offences of all those of that society; there, and there only, is political society, where every one of the members hath quitted this natural power, resigned it up into the hands of the community in all cases that exclude him not from appealing for protection to the law established by it. And thus all private judgment of every particular member being excluded, the community comes to be umpire, by settled, standing rules, indifferent, and the same to all parties; and by men having authority from the community for the execution of those rules,[4] decides all the differences that may happen between any members of that society concerning any matter of right, and punishes those offences which any member hath committed against the society, with such penalties as the law has established; whereby it is easy to discern who are and who are not in political society together. Those who are united into one body, and have a common established law and judicature to appeal to, with authority to decide controversies between them and punish offenders, are in civil society one with another; but those who have no such common appeal—I mean on earth—are still in the state of nature, each being, where there is no other, judge for himself and executioner, which is, as I have before shewn it, the perfect state of nature.

88. And thus the commonwealth comes by a power to set down what punishment shall belong to the several transgressions which they think worthy of it, committed amongst the members of that society (which is the power of making laws) as well as it has the power to punish any injury done unto any of its members by any one that is not of it (which is the power of war and peace); and all this for the preservation of the property of all the members of that society as far as is possible. But though every man who has entered into civil society, and is become a member of any commonwealth, has thereby quitted[5] his power to punish offences against the law of nature in prosecution of his own private judgment, yet with the judgment of offences, which he has given up to the legislative in all cases where he can appeal to the magistrate, he has given a right to the commonwealth to employ his force for the execution of the judgments of the commonwealth whenever he shall be called to it; which, indeed, are his own judgments, they being made by himself or his representative. And herein we have the original of the

---

4. 2nd edition. 1st edition reads: ". . . umpire; and by understanding indifferent rules and men authorized by the community for their execution, decides . . ."

5. Collected edition. Earlier editions read: ". . . every man entered into society has quitted . . ."

legislative and executive power of civil society, which is to judge by standing laws how far offences are to be punished when committed within the commonwealth, and also to determine[6] by occasional judgments founded on the present circumstances of the fact, how far injuries from without are to be vindicated; and in both these to employ all the force of all the members when there shall be need.

89. Wherever, therefore, any number of men are so united[7] into one society, as to quit every one his executive power of the law of nature, and to resign it to the public, there, and there only, is a political, or civil society. And this is done wherever any number of men, in the state of nature, enter into society to make one people, one body politic, under one supreme government, or else when any one joins himself to, and incorporates with, any government already made. For hereby he authorizes the society, or, which is all one, the legislative thereof, to make laws for him, as the public good of the society shall require, to the execution whereof his own assistance (as to his own decrees) is due. And this puts men out of a state of nature into that of a commonwealth, by setting up a judge on earth with authority to determine all the controversies and redress the injuries that may happen to any member of the commonwealth; which judge is the legislative, or magistrates appointed by it. And wherever there are any number of men, however associated, that have no such decisive power to appeal to, there they are still in the state of nature.

90. Hence it is evident that absolute monarchy, which by some men is counted the only government in the world, is indeed inconsistent with civil society, and so can be no form of civil government at all. For the end of civil society being to avoid and remedy those inconveniencies of the state of nature which necessarily follow from every man's being judge in his own case, by setting up a known authority to which every one of that society may appeal upon any injury received or controversy that may arise, and which every one of the society ought to obey*; wherever any persons are, who have not such an authority to appeal to and decide any difference between them, there those persons are still in the state of nature. And so is every absolute prince, in respect of those who are under his dominion.

91. For he being supposed to have all, both legislative and executive,

---

6. "To determine" added in collected edition.

7. 2nd edition. 1st edition reads: ". . . of men so unite . . ."

*"The public power of all society is above every soul contained in the same society, and the principal use of that power is to give laws unto all that are under it, which laws in such cases we must obey, unless there be reason shewed which may necessarily enforce that the law of reason or of God doth enjoin the contrary."—Hooker. (*Eccl. Pol.*, lib. i, sect. 16).

power in himself alone, there is no judge to be found; no appeal lies open to any one who may fairly and indifferently and with authority decide, and from whose decision[8] relief and address may be expected of any injury or inconvenience that may be suffered from the prince[9] or by his order; so that such a man, however entitled—Czar, or Grand Seignior, or how you please—is as much in the state of nature, with all under his dominion, as he is with the rest of mankind. For wherever any two men are, who have no standing rule and common judge to appeal to on earth for the determination of controversies of right betwixt them, there they are still in the state of nature,* and under all the inconveniencies of it, with only this woeful difference to the subject, or rather slave, of an absolute prince: that, whereas in the ordinary state of nature he has a liberty to judge of his right, and according to the best of his power to maintain it; now, whenever his property is invaded by the will and order of his monarch, he has not only no appeal, as those in society ought to have, but, as if he were degraded from the common state of rational creatures, is denied a liberty to judge of or to defend his right; and so is exposed to all the misery and inconveniencies that a man can fear from one who, being in the unrestrained state of nature, is yet corrupted with flattery, and armed with power.

92. For he that thinks absolute power purifies men's blood, and corrects the baseness of human nature, need read but the history of this or any other age, to be convinced of the contrary. He that would have been insolent and injurious in the woods of America, would not probably be much better in a throne; where, perhaps, learning and religion shall be found out to justify all that he shall do to his subjects, and the sword presently silence all those that dare question it. For what the protection of absolute monarchy is, what kind of fathers of their countries

---

8. Collected edition. Earlier editions read: ". . . from whence relief . . ."

9. The prince: collected edition. Earlier editions read: "him."

*"To take away all such mutual grievances, injuries, and wrongs, *i.e.*, such as attend men in the state of nature, there was no way but only by growing into composition and agreement amongst themselves by ordaining some kind of government public, and by yielding themselves subject thereunto, that unto whom they granted authority to rule and govern, by them the peace, tranquillity, and happy estate of the rest might be procured. Men always knew that where force and injury was offered, they might be defenders of themselves. They knew that, however men may seek their own commodity, yet if this were done with injury unto others, it was not to be suffered, but by all men and all good means to be withstood. Finally, they knew that no man might, in reason, take upon him to determine his own right, and according to his own determination proceed in maintenance thereof, in as much as every man is towards himself, and them whom he greatly affects, partial; and therefore, that strifes and troubles would be endless, except they gave their common consent, all to be ordered by some whom they should agree upon, without which consent there would be no reason that one man should take upon him to be lord or judge over another."—Hooker (*ibid.*, sect. 10).

it makes princes to be, and to what a degree of happiness and security it carries civil society, where this sort of government is grown to perfection, he that will look into the late relation of Ceylon may easily see.

93. In absolute monarchies, indeed, as well as other governments of the world, the subjects have an appeal to the law and judges, to decide any controversies and restrain any violence that may happen betwixt the subjects themselves, one amongst another. This every one thinks necessary, and believes he deserves to be thought a declared enemy to society and mankind who should go about to take it away. But whether this be from a true love of mankind and society, and such a charity as we owe all one to another, there is reason to doubt. For this is no more than what every man who loves his own power, profit, or greatness may, and naturally must do, keep those animals from hurting or destroying one another who labour and drudge only for his pleasure and advantage; and so are taken care of, not out of any love the master has for them, but love of himself, and the profit they bring him. For if it be asked, what security, what fence is there, in such a state, against the violence and oppression of this absolute ruler, the very question can scarce be borne. They are ready to tell you that it deserves death only to ask after safety. Betwixt subject and subject, they will grant, there must be measures, laws and judges, for their mutual peace and security; but as for the ruler, he ought to be absolute, and is above all such circumstances; because he has power to do more hurt and wrong, 'tis right when he does it. To ask how you may be guarded from harm or injury on that side where the strongest hand is to do it, is presently the voice of faction and rebellion. As if when men quitting the state of nature entered into society, they agreed that all of them but one should be under the restraint of laws, but that he should still retain all the liberty of the state of nature, increased with power, and made licentious by impunity. This is to think that men are so foolish that they take care to avoid what mischiefs may be done them by polecats or foxes, but are content, nay, think it safety, to be devoured by lions.

94. But, whatever flatterers may talk to amuse people's understanding, it hinders[10] not men from feeling; and when they perceive that any man, in what station soever, is out of the bounds of the civil society which[11] they are of, and that they have no appeal on earth against any harm they may receive from him, they are apt to think themselves in the state of nature in respect of him whom they find to be so; and to take care, as soon as they can, to have that safety and security in civil society for which it was first instituted, and for which only they entered

---

10. *Errata* list in 2nd edition. 1st edition reads: "it never hinders . . ."
11. "Which" added in collected edition.

into it. And, therefore, though perhaps at first (as shall be shewn more at large hereafter in the following part of this discourse), some one good and excellent man, having got a pre-eminency amongst the rest, had this deference paid to his goodness and virtue, as to a kind of natural authority, that the chief rule, with arbitration of their differences, by a tacit consent devolved into his hands, without any other caution but the assurance they had of his uprightness and wisdom; yet when time, giving authority and (as some men would persuade us) sacredness of customs which the negligent and unforeseeing innocence of the first ages began, had brought in successors of another stamp, the people finding their properties not secure under the government, as then it was (whereas government has no other end but the preservation of property),*could never be safe nor at rest, nor think themselves in civil society, till the legislature[12]was placed in collective bodies of men, call them senate, parliament, or what you please. By which means every single person became subject, equally with other the meanest men, to those laws, which he himself, as part of the legislative, had established; nor could any one by his own authority avoid the force of the law when once made, nor by any pretence of superiority plead exemption, thereby to license his own, or the miscarriages of any of his dependents. No man in civil society can be exempted from the laws of it.[†] For if any man may do what he thinks fit, and there be no appeal on earth for redress or security against any harm he shall do, I ask whether he be not perfectly still in the state of nature, and so can be no part or member of that civil society; unless any one will say the state of nature and civil society are one and the same thing, which I have never yet found any one so great a patron of anarchy as to affirm.

---

12. Legislature: collected edition. Earlier editions read: "legislative."

*"At the first, when some certain kind of regiment was once appointed, it may be that nothing was then farther thought upon for the manner of governing, but all permitted unto their wisdom and discretion which were to rule till, by experience, they found this for all parts very inconvenient, so as the thing which they had devised for a remedy did indeed but increase the sore which it should have cured. They saw that to live by one man's will became the cause of all men's misery. This constrained them to come unto laws wherein all men might see their duty beforehand, and know the penalties of transgressing them."—Hooker (Eccl. Pol., lib. i, sect. 10).

[†]"Civil law, being the act of the whole body politic, doth therefore overrule each several part of the same body."—Hooker (ibid.).

Chapter VIII

Of the Beginning of Political Societies

95. Men being, as has been said, by nature all free, equal, and independent, no one can be put out of this estate, and subjected to the political power of another, without his own consent. The only way whereby any one divests himself of his natural liberty and puts on the bonds of civil society is by agreeing[1] with other men to join and unite into a community for their comfortable, safe, and peaceable living one amongst another, in a secure enjoyment of their properties, and a greater security against any that are not of it. This any number of men may do, because it injures not the freedom of the rest; they are left as they were in the liberty of the state of nature. When any number of men have so consented to make one community or government, they are thereby presently incorporated, and make one body politic, wherein the majority have a right to act and conclude the rest.

96. For when any number of men have, by the consent of every individual, made a community, they have thereby made that community one body, with a power to act as one body, which is only by the will and determination of the majority. For that which acts any community being only the consent of the individuals of it, and it being necessary to that which is one body to move[2] one way, it is necessary the body should move that way whither the greater force carries it, which is the consent of the majority; or else it is impossible it should act or continue one body, one community, which the consent of every individual that united into it agreed that it should; and so every one is bound by that consent to be concluded by the majority. And therefore we see that in assemblies empowered to act by positive laws, where no number is set by that positive law which empowers them, the act of the majority passes for the act of the whole, and of course determines, as having by the law of nature and reason the power of the whole.

97. And thus every man, by consenting with others to make one body politic under one government, puts himself under an obligation to every one of that society, to submit to the determination of the majority, and to be concluded by it; or else this original compact, whereby he with others incorporates into one society, would signify nothing, and be no compact, if he be left free and under no other ties than he was in before in the state of nature. For what appearance would there be of

---

1. Altered in collected edition. Earlier editions read: ". . . his own consent, which is done by agreeing . . ."

2. Altered in collected edition. Earlier editions read: ". . . it being one body must move one way . . ."

any compact? What new engagement if he were no farther tied by any decrees of the society, than he himself thought fit, and did actually consent to? This would be still as great a liberty as he himself had before his compact, or any one else in the state of nature hath, who may submit himself and consent to any acts of it if he thinks fit.

98. For if the consent of the majority shall not in reason be received as the act of the whole, and conclude every individual, nothing but the consent of every individual can make anything to be the act of the whole, but such a consent is next to impossible ever to be had, if we consider[3] the infirmities of health and avocations of business, which in a number, though much less than that of a commonwealth, will necessarily keep many away from the public assembly. To which if we add the variety of opinions, and contrariety of interests, which unavoidably happen in all collections of men, the coming into society upon such terms would be only[4] like Cato's coming into the theatre, *tantum et exiret*.[5] Such a constitution as this would make the mighty Leviathan of a shorter duration than the feeblest creatures, and not let it outlast the day it was born in; which cannot be supposed, till we can think that rational creatures should desire and constitute societies only to be dissolved. For where the majority cannot conclude the rest, there they cannot act as one body, and consequently will be immediately dissolved again.

99. Whosoever therefore out of a state of nature unite into a community must be understood to give up all the power necessary to the ends for which they unite into society, to the majority of the community, unless they expressly agreed in any number greater than the majority. And this is done by barely agreeing to unite into one political society, which is all the compact that is, or needs be, between the individuals that enter into or make up a commonwealth. And thus that which begins and actually constitutes any political society is nothing but the consent of any number of freemen capable of a majority to unite and incorporate into such a society. And this is that, and that only, which did or could give beginning to any lawful government in the world.

100. To this I find two objections made.

---

3. Altered in collected edition. Earlier editions read: ". . . of the whole, which considering the infirmities . . ."

4. Altered in collected edition. Earlier editions read: ". . . public assembly; and the variety of opinions, and contrariety of interests, which unavoidably happen in all collections of men, 'tis next impossible ever to be had. And therefore if coming into society be upon such terms it will be only like Cato's . . ."

5. I leave the Latin, which appeared in the earlier editions; but the collected edition altered this to "only to go out again."

First: That there are no instances to be found in story of a company of men, independent and equal one amongst another, that met together, and in this way began and set up a government.

Secondly: 'Tis impossible of right that men should do so, because all men being born under government, they are to submit to that, and are not at liberty to begin a new one.

101. To the first there is this to answer: That it is not at all to be wondered that history gives us but a very little account of men that lived together in the state of nature. The inconveniencies of that condition, and the love and want of society, no sooner brought any number of them together, but they presently united and incorporated if they designed to continue together. And if we may not suppose men ever to have been in the state of nature, because we hear not much of them in such a state, we may as well suppose the armies of Salmanasser or Xerxes were never children, because we hear little of them till they were men, and embodied in armies. Government is everywhere antecedent to records, and letters seldom come in amongst a people, till a long continuation of civil society has, by other more necessary arts, provided for their safety, ease, and plenty. And then they begin to look after the history of their founders, and search into their original, when they have outlived the memory of it. For 'tis with commonwealths as with particular persons, they are commonly ignorant of their own birth and infancies. And if they know anything of their original, they are beholden for it to the accidental records that others have kept of it. And those that we have of the beginning of any polities in the world, excepting that of the Jews, where God himself immediately interposed, and which favours not at all paternal dominion, are all either plain instances of such a beginning as I have mentioned, or at least have manifest footsteps of it.

102. He must shew a strange inclination to deny evident matter of fact when it agrees not with his hypothesis, who will not allow that the beginning of Rome and Venice were by the uniting together of several men free and independent one of another, amongst whom there was no natural superiority or subjection. And if Josephus Acosta's word may be taken, he tells us that in many parts of America there was no government at all. "There are great and apparent conjectures," says he, "that these men," speaking of those of Peru, "for a long time had neither kings nor commonwealths, but lived in troops, as they do this day in Florida, the Cheriquanas, those of Brazil, and many other nations, which have no certain kings, but as occasion is offered in peace or war, they choose their captains as they please" (l. i, c. 25). If it be said that every man there was born subject to his father, or the head of his family, that the subjection due from a child to a father took not away his

freedom of uniting into what political society he thought fit, has been already proved. But be that as it will, these men, 'tis evident, were actually free; and whatever superiority some politicians now would place in any of them, they themselves claimed it not; but by consent were all equal, till by the same consent they set rulers over themselves. So that their politic societies all began from a voluntary union, and the mutual agreement of men freely acting in the choice of their governors and forms of government.

103. And I hope those who went away from Sparta with Palantus, mentioned by Justin, l. iii, c. 4, will be allowed to have been freemen, independent one of another, and to have set up a government over themselves, by their own consent. Thus I have given several examples out of history of people free and in the state of nature that, being met together, incorporated and began a commonwealth. And if the want of such instances be an argument to prove that government were not nor could not be so begun, I suppose the contenders for paternal empire were better let it alone than urge it against natural liberty. For if they can give so many instances, out of history, of governments begun upon paternal right, I think (though at best an argument from what has been, to what should of right be, has no great force) one might, without any great danger, yield them the cause. But if I might advise them in the case, they would do well not to search too much into the original of governments as they have begun *de facto*, lest they should find at the foundation of most of them something very little favourable to the design they promote and such a power as they contend for.

104. But to conclude, reason being plain on our side that men are naturally free, and the examples of history shewing that the governments of the world, that were begun in peace, had their beginning laid on that foundation, and were made by the consent of the people, there can be little room for doubt, either where the right is, or what has been the opinion or practice of mankind, about the first erecting of governments.

105. I will not deny, that if we look back as far as history will direct us, towards the original of commonwealths, we shall generally find them under the government and administration of one man. And I am also apt to believe that where a family was numerous enough to subsist by itself, and continued entire together, without mixing with others, as it often happens where there is much land and few people, the government commonly began in the father. For the father having, by the law of nature, the same power with every man else to punish as he thought fit any offences against that law, might thereby punish his transgressing children, even when they were men, and out of their pupilage; and they were very likely to submit to his punishment, and all

join with him against the offender, in their turns, giving him thereby power to execute his sentence against any transgression, and so in effect make him the lawmaker and governor over all that remained in conjunction with his family. He was fittest to be trusted; paternal affection secured their property and interest under his care; and the custom of obeying him in their childhood made it easier to submit to him rather than to any other. If therefore they must have one to rule them, as government is hardly to be avoided amongst men that live together, who so likely to be the man as he that was their common father; unless negligence, cruelty, or any other defect of mind or body, made him unfit for it? But when either the father died, and left his next heir, for want of age, wisdom, courage, or any other qualities, less fit for rule; or where several families met and consented to continue together, there 'tis not to be doubted but they used their natural freedom to set up him whom they judged the ablest and most likely to rule well over them. Conformable hereunto we find the people of America, who (living out of the reach of the conquering swords and spreading domination of the two great empires of Peru and Mexico) enjoyed their own natural freedom, though, *cœteris paribus*, they commonly prefer the heir of their deceased king; yet if they find him any way weak or uncapable, they pass him by and set up the stoutest and bravest man for their ruler.

106. Thus, though looking back as far as records give us any account of peopling the world, and the history of nations, we commonly find the government to be in one hand; yet it destroys not that which I affirm, *viz.*, that the beginning of politic society depends upon the consent of the individuals to join into and make one society; who, when they are thus incorporated, might set up what form of government they thought fit. But this having given occasion to men to mistake, and think that by nature government was monarchical, and belonged to the father, it may not be amiss here to consider why people in the beginning generally pitched upon this form, which, though perhaps the father's pre-eminence might in the first institution of some commonwealths give a rise to, and place in the beginning, the power in one hand; yet it is plain that the reason that continued the form of government in a single person was not any regard or respect to paternal authority, since all petty monarchies, that is, almost all monarchies, near their original, have been commonly—at least upon occasion—elective.

107. First then, in the beginning of things, the father's government of the childhood of those sprung from him having accustomed them to the rule of one man, and taught them that where it was exercised with care and skill, with affection and love to those under it, it was sufficient to procure and preserve to men all the political happiness they sought for in society. It was no wonder that they should pitch upon and natu-

rally run into that form of government, which from their infancy they had been all accustomed to, and which, by experience, they had found both easy and safe. To which if we add, that monarchy being simple and most obvious to men whom neither experience had instructed in forms of government, nor the ambition or insolence of empire had taught to beware of the encroachments of prerogative, or the inconveniencies of absolute power, which monarchy in succession was apt to lay claim to, and bring upon them; it was not at all strange that they should not much trouble themselves to think of methods of restraining any exorbitances of those to whom they had given the authority over them, and of balancing the power of government, by placing several parts of it in different hands. They had neither felt the oppression of tyrannical dominion, nor did the fashion of the age, nor their possessions or way of living (which afforded little matter for covetousness or ambition), give them any reason to apprehend or provide against it; and therefore 'tis no wonder they put themselves into such a frame of government as was not only, as I said, most obvious and simple, but also best suited to their present state and condition, which stood more in need of defence against foreign invasions and injuries than of multiplicity of laws. The equality of a simple poor way of living, confining their desires within the bounds of each man's small property, made few controversies, and so no need of many laws to decide them, or variety of officers to superintend the process or look after the execution of justice,[6] where there were but few trespasses and few offenders. Since, then, those who liked one another so well as to join into society, cannot but be supposed to have some acquaintance and friendship together, and some trust one in another, they could not but have greater apprehensions of others than of one another; and therefore their first care and thought cannot but be supposed to be how to secure themselves against foreign force. 'Twas natural for them to put themselves under a frame of government which might best serve to that end, and choose the wisest and bravest man to conduct them in their wars, and lead them out against their enemies, and in this chiefly be their ruler.

108. Thus we see that the kings of the Indians in America—which is still a pattern of the first ages in Asia and Europe whilst the inhabitants were too few for the country, and want of people and money gave men no temptation to enlarge their possessions of land, or contest for wider extent of ground—are little more than generals of their armies; and though they command absolutely in war, yet at home and in time of peace they exercise very little dominion, and have but a very moderate

---

6. Altered in collected edition. Earlier editions read: ". . . multiplicity of laws, where there was but very little property; and wanted not variety of rulers and abundance of officers to direct and look after their execution, where there were but few . . ."

sovereignty, the resolutions of peace and war being ordinarily either in the people or in a council. Though the war itself, which admits not of plurality of governors, naturally devolves the command into the king's sole authority.

109. And thus in Israel itself, the chief business of their judges and first kings seems to have been to be captains of war, and leaders of their armies; which (besides what is signified by going out and in before the people, which was, to march forth to war, and home again in the heads of their forces) appears plainly in the story of Jephtha. The Ammonites making war upon Israel, the Gileadites in fear send to Jephtha, a bastard of their family whom they had cast off, and article with him, if he will assist them against the Ammonites, to make him their ruler; which they do in these words: "And the people made him head and captain over them" (Judges xi. 11), which was, as it seems, all one as to be judge. "And he judged Israel" (Judges xii. 7), that is, was their captain-general, six years. So when Jotham upbraids the Shechemites with the obligation they had to Gideon, who had been their judge and ruler, he tells them "He fought for you, and adventured his life for, and delivered you out of the hands of Midian" (Judges ix. 17). Nothing mentioned of him but what he did as a general; and indeed that is all is found in his history, or in any of the rest of the judges. And Abimelech particularly is called king, though at most he was but their general. And when, being weary of the ill-conduct of Samuel's sons, the children of Israel desired a king "like all the nations, to judge them and to go out before them, and to fight their battles" (1 Sam. viii. 20), God, granting their desire, says to Samuel: "I will send thee a man, and thou shalt anoint him to be captain over my people Israel, that he may save my people out of the hands of the Philistines" (ix. 16). As if the only business of a king had been to lead out their armies, and fight in their defence; and accordingly at his inauguration pouring a vial of oil upon him, declares to Saul that "the Lord had anointed him to be captain over his inheritance" (x. 1). And, therefore, those who, after Saul's being solemnly chosen and saluted king by the tribes at Mizpah, were unwilling to have him their king, make no other objection but this: "How shall this man save us?" (verse 27) as if they should have said, "This man is unfit to be our king, not having skill and conduct enough in war to be able to defend us." And when God resolved to transfer the government to David, it is in these words: "But now thy kingdom shall not continue. The Lord hath sought him a man after his own heart, and the Lord hath commanded him to be captain over his people" (xiii. 4). As if the whole kingly authority were nothing else but to be their general; and, therefore, the tribes who had stuck to Saul's family, and opposed David's reign, when they came to Hebron with terms of

submission to him, they tell him, amongst other arguments, they had to submit to him as to their king, that he was, in effect, their king in Saul's time, and therefore, they had no reason but to receive him as their king now. "Also," say they, "in time past, when Saul was king over us, thou wast he that leddest out and broughtest in Israel, and the Lord said unto thee, 'Thou shalt feed my people Israel, and thou shalt be a captain over Israel.'"

110. Thus, whether a family by degrees grew up into a common-wealth, and the fatherly authority being continued on to the elder son, every one in his turn growing up under it, tacitly submitted to it; and the easiness and equality of it not offending any one, every one acquiesced, till time seemed to have confirmed it, and settled a right of succession by prescription; or whether several families, or the descendants of several families, whom chance, neighbourhood, or business brought together, uniting[7] into society, the need of a general, whose conduct might defend them against their enemies in war, and the great confidence the innocency and sincerity of that poor but virtuous age (such as are almost all those which begin governments that ever come to last in the world) gave men one of another, made the first beginners of commonwealths generally put the rule into one man's hand, without any other express limitation or restraint, but what the nature of the thing and the end of government required. Whichever of those it was that at first put the rule into the hands of a single person, certain it is nobody was entrusted with it but for the public good[8] and safety, and to those ends, in the infancies of commonwealths, those who had it commonly used it. And unless they[9] had done so, young societies could not have subsisted. Without such nursing fathers, tender and careful of the public weal,[10] all governments would have sunk under the weakness and infirmities of their infancy, and the prince and people had soon perished together.

111. But though[11] the golden age (before vain ambition, and *amor sceleratus habendi*, evil concupiscence, had corrupted men's minds into a mistake of true power and honour) had more virtue, and consequently better governors, as well as less vicious subjects; and there was then no

---

7. Uniting: collected edition. Earlier editions read "united."

8. Altered in collected edition. Earlier editions read: ". . . government required. It was given them for the public good . . ."

9. 6th edition. Collected edition reads: ". . . commonwealths, commonly used it. And unless those who had it had done so . . ." Earlier editions read: ". . . commonwealths, they commonly used it, and unless they had done so . . ."

10. Altered in collected edition. Earlier editions read: ". . . nursing fathers; without this care of the governors, all governments . . ."

11. Corrected in 2nd edition. 1st edition reads: "But the golden age (though before . . ."

stretching prerogative, on the one side, to oppress the people, nor consequently, on the other, any dispute about privilege, to lessen or restrain the power of the magistrate, and so no contest betwixt rulers and people about governors or government.* Yet, when ambition and luxury in future ages would retain and increase the power, without doing the business for which it was given, and, aided by flattery, taught princes to have distinct and separate interests from their people, men found it necessary to examine more carefully the original and rights of government, and to find out ways to restrain the exorbitances and prevent the abuses of that power which, they having entrusted in another's hands only for their own good, they found was made use of to hurt them.

112. Thus we may see how probable it is that people that were naturally free, and by their own consent either submitted to the government of their father, or united together out of different families to make a government, should generally put the rule into one man's hands, and choose to be under the conduct of a single person, without so much as by express conditions limiting or regulating his power, which they thought safe enough in his honesty and prudence, though they never dreamt of monarchy being *jure divino*, which we never heard of among mankind till it was revealed to us by the divinity of this last age; nor ever allowed paternal power to have a right to dominion, or to be the foundation of all government. And thus much may suffice to show that, as far as we have any light from history, we have reason to conclude that all peaceful beginnings of government have been laid in the consent of the people. I say peaceful, because I shall have occasion in another place to speak of conquest, which some esteem a way of beginning of governments.

The other objection I find urged against the beginning of polities in the way I have mentioned is this, *viz.*:

113. That all men being born under government, some or other, it is impossible any of them should ever be free and at liberty to unite together and begin a new one, or ever be able to erect a lawful government.

If this argument be good, I ask, how came so many lawful monarchies into the world? For if anybody, upon this supposition, can show

---

*"At first, when some certain kind of regiment was once approved, it may be nothing was then farther thought upon for the manner of governing, but all permitted unto their wisdom and discretion, which were to rule, till by experience they found this for all parts very inconvenient, so as the thing which they had devised for a remedy did indeed but increase the sore which it should have cured. They saw that to live by one man's will became the cause of all men's misery. This constrained them to come unto laws wherein all men might see their duty beforehand and know the penalties of transgressing them."—Hooker (*Eccl. Pol.*, lib. i, sect. 10).

me any one man, in any age of the world, free to begin a lawful monarchy, I will be bound to show him ten other free men at liberty at the same time to unite and begin a new government under a regal, or any other form; it being demonstration that if any one, born under the dominion of another, may be so free as to have a right to command others in a new and distinct empire, every one that is born under the dominion of another may be so free too, and may become a ruler or subject of a distinct separate government. And so by this their own principle either all men, however born, are free, or else there is but one lawful prince, one lawful government in the world. And then they have nothing to do but barely to shew us which that is; which, when they have done, I doubt not but all mankind will easily agree to pay obedience to him.

114. Though it be a sufficient answer to their objection to shew that it involves them in the same difficulties that it doth those they use it against, yet I shall endeavour to discover the weakness of this argument a little farther.

"All men," say they, "are born under government, and therefore they cannot be at liberty to begin a new one. Every one is born a subject to his father, or his prince, and is therefore under the perpetual tie of subjection and allegiance." 'Tis plain mankind never owned nor considered any such natural subjection that they were born in, to one or to the other that tied them without their own consents, to a subjection to them and their heirs.

115. For there are no examples so frequent in history, both sacred and profane, as those of men withdrawing themselves and their obedience from the jurisdiction they were born under, and the family or community they were bred up in, and setting up new governments in other places; from whence sprang all that number of petty commonwealths in the beginning of ages, and which always multiplied, as long as there was room enough, till the stronger or more fortunate swallowed the weaker; and those great ones again breaking to pieces, dissolved into lesser dominions. All which are so many testimonies against paternal sovereignty, and plainly prove that it was not the natural right of the father descending to his heirs that made governments in the beginning, since it was impossible upon that ground there should have been so many little kingdoms; all must have been[12] but only one universal monarchy, if men had not been at liberty to separate themselves from their families and the[13] government, be it what it will, that was set

---

12. Altered in collected edition. Earlier editions read: "little kingdoms, but only one universal . . ."

13. "Their" corrected to "the" in *errata* list in 2nd edition.

up in it, and go and make distinct commonwealths and other governments as they thought fit.

116. This has been the practice of the world from its first beginning to this day; nor is it now any more hindrance to the freedom of mankind that they are born under constituted and ancient polities that have established laws and set forms of government, than if they were born in the woods amongst the unconfined inhabitants that run loose in them. For those who would persuade us that by being born under any government we are naturally subjects to it, and have no more any title or pretence to the freedom of the state of nature, have no other reason (bating that of paternal power, which we have already answered) to produce for it, but only because our fathers or progenitors passed away their natural liberty, and thereby bound up themselves and their posterity to a perpetual subjection to the government which they themselves submitted to. 'Tis true that whatever engagements or promises any one has made for himself, he is under the obligation of them, but cannot by any compact whatsoever bind his children or posterity. For his son when a man being altogether as free as his father, any act of the father can no more give away the liberty of the son than it can of anybody else. He may indeed annex such conditions to the land he enjoyed as a subject of any commonwealth as may oblige his son to be of that community, if he will enjoy those possessions which were his father's, because that estate being his father's property he may dispose or settle it as he pleases.

117. And this has generally given the occasion to mistake in this matter, because commonwealths not permitting any part of their dominions to be dismembered, nor to be enjoyed by any but those of their community, the son cannot ordinarily enjoy the possessions of his father but under the same terms his father did, by becoming a member of the society; whereby he puts himself presently under the government he finds there established, as much as any other subject of that commonwealth. And thus the consent of freemen, born under government, which only makes them members of it, being given separately in their turns, as each comes to be of age, and not in a multitude together, people take no notice of it, and thinking it not done at all, or not necessary, conclude they are naturally subjects as they are men.

118. But 'tis plain governments themselves understand it otherwise; they claim no power over the son, because of that they had over the father; nor look on children as being their subjects by their father's being so. If a subject of England have a child by an English woman in France, whose subject is he? Not the King of England's, for he must have leave to be admitted to the privileges of it; nor the King of France's, for how then has his father a liberty to bring him away and

breed him as he pleases? And whoever was judged as a traitor or deserter, if he left or warred against a country, for being barely born in it of parents that were aliens there? 'Tis plain then by the practice of governments themselves, as well as by the law of right reason, that a child is born a subject of no country or government. He is under his father's tuition and authority till he comes to age of discretion, and then he is a freeman, at liberty what government he will put himself under, what body politic he will unite himself to. For if an Englishman's son, born in France, be at liberty, and may do so, 'tis evident there is no tie upon him by his father's being a subject of this kingdom; nor is he bound up by any compact of his ancestors. And why then hath not his son by the same reason, the same liberty, though he be born anywhere else? Since the power that a father hath naturally over his children is the same wherever they be born, and the ties of natural obligations are not bounded by the positive limits of kingdoms and commonwealths.

119. Every man being, as has been shewn, naturally free, and nothing being able to put him into subjection to any earthly power but only his own consent, it is to be considered what shall be understood to be a sufficient declaration of a man's consent to make him subject to the laws of any government. There is a common distinction of an express and a tacit consent, which will concern our present case. Nobody doubts but an express consent of any man entering into any society makes him a perfect member of that society, a subject of that government. The difficulty is, what ought to be looked upon as a tacit consent, and how far it binds, *i.e.*, how far any one shall be looked on to have consented, and thereby submitted to any government, where he has made no expressions of it at all. And to this I say that every man that hath any possessions,[14] or enjoyment of any part of the dominions of any government, doth thereby give his tacit consent, and is as far forth obliged to obedience to the laws of that government during such enjoyment as any one under it; whether this his possession be of land to him and his heirs for ever, or a lodging only for a week; or whether it be barely travelling freely on the highway; and in effect it reaches as far as the very being of any one within the territories of that government.

120. To understand this the better, it is fit to consider that every man when he at first incorporates himself into any commonwealth, he, by his uniting himself thereunto, annexes also, and submits to the community, those possessions which he has or shall acquire that do not already belong to any other government; for it would be a direct contradiction for any one to enter into society with others for the securing and regulating of property, and yet to suppose his land, whose property is to be regu-

---

14. "Possessions" in collected edition. Earlier editions read: "possession."

lated by the laws of the society, should be exempt from the jurisdiction of that government to which he himself, the proprietor[15] of the land, is a subject. By the same act, therefore, whereby any one unites his person, which was before free, to any commonwealth, by the same he unites his possessions, which were before free, to it also; and they become, both of them, person and possession, subject to the government and dominion of that commonwealth as long as it hath a being. Whoever therefore from thenceforth by inheritance, purchases, permission, or otherwise, enjoys any part of the land so annexed to, and under the government of that commonwealth, must take it with the condition it is under, that is, of submitting to the government of the commonwealth under whose jurisdiction it is, as far forth as any subject of it.

121. But since the government has a direct jurisdiction only over the land, and reaches the possessor of it (before he has actually incorporated himself in the society), only as he dwells upon, and enjoys that: the obligation any one is under, by virtue of such enjoyment, to submit to the government, begins and ends with the enjoyment; so that whenever the owner, who has given nothing but such a tacit consent to the government, will by donation, sale, or otherwise, quit the said possession, he is at liberty to go and incorporate himself into any other commonwealth, or to agree with others to begin a new one, *in vacuis locis*, in any part of the world they can find free and unpossessed. Whereas he that has once by actual agreement and any express declaration given his consent to be of any commonwealth is perpetually and indispensably obliged to be and remain unalterably a subject to it, and can never be again in the liberty of the state of nature; unless, by any calamity, the government he was under comes to be dissolved, or else by some public acts cuts him off from being any longer a member of it.

122. But submitting to the laws of any country, living quietly and enjoying privileges and protection under them, makes not a man a member of that society. This is only a local protection and homage due to and from all those who, not being in the state of war, come within the territories belonging to any government, to all parts whereof the force of its law extends. But this no more makes a man a member of that society, a perpetual subject of that commonwealth, than it would make a man a subject to another in whose family he found it convenient to abide for some time; though whilst he continued in it he were obliged to comply with the laws, and submit to the government he found there. And thus we see, that foreigners by living all their lives under another government, and enjoying the privileges and protection of it, though

---

15. Corrected in *errata* list in 2nd edition. 1st edition reads: ". . . he himself, and the property of the land . . ."

they are bound even in conscience to submit to its administration as far forth as any denizen, yet do not thereby come to be subjects or members of that commonwealth. Nothing can make any man so, but his actually entering into it by positive engagement, and express promise and compact. This is that which I think concerning the beginning of political societies, and that consent which makes any one a member of any commonwealth.

Chapter IX

Of the Ends of Political Society and Government

123. If man in the state of nature be so free, as has been said; if he be absolute lord of his own person and possessions, equal to the greatest, and subject to nobody, why will he part with his freedom? Why will he give up[1] this empire, and subject himself to the dominion and control of any other power? To which 'tis obvious to answer, that though in the state of nature he hath such a right, yet the enjoyment of it is very uncertain, and constantly exposed to the invasion of others. For all being kings as much as he, every man his equal, and the greater part no strict observers of equity and justice, the enjoyment of the property he has in this state is very unsafe, very unsecure. This makes him willing to quit a condition,[2] which, however free, is full of fears and continual dangers; and 'tis not without reason that he seeks out and is willing to join in society with others, who are already united, or have a mind to unite, for the mutual preservation of their lives, liberties, and estates, which I call by the general name, property.

124. The great and chief end, therefore, of men's uniting into commonwealths, and putting themselves under government, is the preservation of their property; to which in the state of nature there are many things wanting.

First, There wants an established, settled, known law, received and allowed by common consent to be the standard of right and wrong, and the common measure to decide all controversies between them. For though the law of nature be plain and intelligible to all rational creatures; yet men, being biased by their interest, as well as ignorant for want of study of it, are not apt to allow of it as a law binding to them in the application of it to their particular cases.

125. Secondly, In the state of nature there wants a known and indif-

---

1. Added in 2nd edition. 1st edition reads: ". . . part with his freedom, this empire . . ."
2. A condition: 6th edition. Earlier editions read: "this condition."

ferent judge, with authority to determine all differences according to the established law. For every one in that state, being both judge and executioner of the law of nature, men being partial to themselves, passion and revenge is very apt to carry them too far, and with too much heat in their own cases, as well as negligence and unconcernedness, to make them too remiss in other men's.

126. Thirdly, In the state of nature there often wants power to back and support the sentence when right, and to give it due execution. They who by any injustice offended will seldom fail, where they are able, by force to make good their injustice; such resistance many times makes the punishment dangerous, and frequently destructive to those who attempt it.

127. Thus mankind, notwithstanding all the privileges of the state of nature, being but in an ill condition while they remain in it, are quickly driven into society. Hence it comes to pass that we seldom find any number of men live any time together in this state. The inconveniencies that they are therein exposed to by the irregular and uncertain exercise of the power every man has of punishing the transgressions of others, make them take sanctuary under the established laws of government, and therein seek the preservation of their property. 'Tis this makes them so willingly give up every one his single power of punishing, to be exercised by such alone, as shall be appointed to it amongst them; and by such rules as the community, or those authorized by them to that purpose, shall agree on. And in this we have the original right and rise of both the legislative and executive power, as well as of the governments and societies themselves.

128. For in the state of nature, to omit the liberty he has of innocent delights, a man has two powers.

The first is to do whatsoever he thinks fit for the preservation of himself and others within the permission of the law of nature, by which law, common to them all, he and all the rest of mankind are of one community, make up one society, distinct from all other creatures. And were it not for the corruption and viciousness of degenerate men there would be no need of any other, no necessity that men should separate from this great and natural community, and by positive agreements combine into smaller and divided associations.[3]

The other power a man has in the state of nature is the power to punish the crimes committed against that law. Both these he gives up when he joins in a private, if I may so call it, or particular political society, and incorporates into any commonwealth separate from the rest of mankind.

---

3. Altered in collected edition. Earlier editions read: ". . . natural community, and associate into lesser combinations."

129. The first power, *viz.*, of doing whatsoever he thought fit for the preservation of himself and the rest of mankind, he gives up to be regulated by laws made by the society, so far forth as the preservation of himself and the rest of that society shall require; which laws of the society in many things confine the liberty he had by the law of nature.

130. Secondly, The power of punishing he wholly gives up, and engages his natural force (which he might before employ in the execution of the law of nature, by his own single authority as he thought fit), to assist the executive power of the society, as the law thereof shall require. For being now in a new state, wherein he is to enjoy many conveniencies, from the labour, assistance, and society of others in the same community, as well as protection from its whole strength; he has to part also with as much of his natural liberty, in providing for himself, as the good, prosperity, and safety of the society shall require; which is not only necessary but just, since the other members of the society do the like.

131. But though men when they enter into society give up the equality, liberty, and executive power they had in the state of nature into the hands of the society, to be so far disposed of by the legislative as the good of the society shall require; yet it being only with an intention in every one the better to preserve himself, his liberty, and property (for no rational creature can be supposed to change his condition with an intention to be worse), the power of the society, or legislative constituted by them, can never be supposed to extend farther than the common good, but is obliged to secure every one's property by providing against those three defects above-mentioned that made the state of nature so unsafe and uneasy. And so whoever has the legislative or supreme power of any commonwealth is bound to govern by established standing laws, promulgated and known to the people, and not by extemporary decrees; by indifferent and upright judges, who are to decide controversies by those laws; and to employ the force of the community at home only in the execution of such laws, or abroad to prevent or redress foreign injuries, and secure the community from inroads and invasion. And all this to be directed to no other end but the peace, safety, and public good of the people.

Chapter X

Of the Forms of a Commonwealth

132. The majority having, as has been shewed, upon men's first uniting into society, the whole power of the community naturally in them, may employ all that power in making laws for the community from

time to time, and executing those laws by officers of their own appointing: and then the form of the government is a perfect democracy; or else may put the power of making laws into the hands of a few select men, and their heirs or successors, and then it is an oligarchy; or else into the hands of one man, and then it is a monarchy; if to him and his heirs, it is an hereditary monarchy; if to him only for life, but upon his death the power only of nominating a successor to return to them, an elective monarchy. And so accordingly of these the community may[1] make compounded and mixed forms of government, as they think good. And if the legislative power be at first given by the majority to one or more persons only for their lives, or any limited time, and then the supreme power to revert to them again; when it is so reverted, the community may dispose of it again anew into what hands they please, and so constitute a new form of government. For the form of government depending upon the placing the supreme power, which is the legislative, it being impossible to conceive that an inferior power should prescribe to a superior, or any but the supreme make laws, according as the power of making laws is placed, such is the form of the commonwealth.

133. By commonwealth, I must be understood all along to mean, not a democracy, or any form of government, but any independent community, which the Latins signified by the word *civitas*, to which the word which best answers in our language is commonwealth, and most properly expresses such a society of men, which community or city in English does not; for there may be subordinate communities in a government, and city amongst us has quite a different notion from commonwealth.[2] And therefore to avoid ambiguity I crave leave to use the word commonwealth in that sense, in which I find it used by King James the First, and I take it[3] to be its genuine signification; which if anybody dislike, I consent with him to change it for a better.

Chapter XI

Of the Extent of the Legislative Power

134. The great end of men's entering into society being the enjoyment of their properties in peace and safety, and the great instrument and

1. The words "the community may" were added in the collected edition.

2. Altered in collected edition. Earlier editions read: ". . . which community does not, for there may be subordinate communities in a government; and city much less. And therefore to avoid . . ."

3. the First, and I take to be: collected edition. 1st edition reads: "himself, which I think to be." "Himself" was altered to "the First" in the 2nd edition.

means of that being the laws established in that society: the first and fundamental positive law of all commonwealths is the establishing of the legislative power; as the first and fundamental natural law, which is to govern even the legislative itself, is the preservation of the society, and (as far as will consist with the public good) of every person in it. This legislative is not only the supreme power of the commonwealth, but sacred and unalterable in the hands where the community have once placed it; nor can any edict of anybody else, in what form soever conceived, or by what power soever backed, have the force and obligation of a law, which has not its sanction from that legislative which the public has chosen and appointed. For without this the law could not have that, which is absolutely necessary to its being a law, the consent of the society, over whom nobody can have a power to make laws,* but by their own consent, and by authority received from them; and therefore all the obedience, which by the most solemn ties any one can be obliged to pay, ultimately terminates in this supreme power, and is directed by those laws which it enacts; nor can any oaths to any foreign power whatsoever, or any domestic subordinate power, discharge any member of the society from his obedience to the legislative, acting pursuant to their trust; nor oblige him to any obedience contrary to the laws so enacted, or farther than they do allow; it being ridiculous to imagine one can be tied ultimately to obey any power in the society which is not the supreme.

135. Though the legislative, whether placed in one or more, whether it be always in being, or only by intervals, though it be the supreme power in every commonwealth, yet,

First, It is not nor can possibly be absolutely arbitrary over the lives and fortunes of the people. For it being but the joint power of every member of the society given up to that person, or assembly, which is legislator; it can be no more than those persons had in a state of nature

---

*"The lawful power of making laws to command whole politic societies of men, belonging so properly unto the same entire societies, that for any prince or potentate, of what kind soever upon earth, to exercise the same of himself, and not by express commission immediately and personally received from God, or else by authority derived at the first from their consent, upon whose persons they impose laws, it is no better than mere tyranny. Laws they are not, therefore, which public approbation hath not made so." — Hooker (*Eccl. Pol.*, lib. i, sect. 10). "Of this point, therefore, we are to note, that sith men naturally have no full and perfect power to command whole politic multitudes of men, therefore utterly without our consent we could in such sort be at no man's commandment living. And to be commanded we do consent, when that society, whereof we be a part, hath at any time before consented, without revoking the same after by the like universal agreement.

"Laws therefore human, of what kind soever, are available by consent." — Hooker (*ibid.*).

before they entered into society, and gave it up to the community. For nobody can transfer to another more power than he has in himself; and nobody has an absolute arbitrary power over himself, or over any other, to destroy his own life, or take away the life or property of another. A man, as has been proved, cannot subject himself to the arbitrary power of another; and having in the state of nature no arbitrary power over the life, liberty, or possession of another, but only so much as the law of nature gave him for the preservation of himself, and the rest of mankind; this is all he doth, or can give up to the commonwealth, and by it to the legislative power, so that the legislative can have no more than this. Their power, in the utmost bounds of it, is limited to the public good of the society.* It is a power that hath no other end but preservation, and therefore can never have a right to destroy, enslave, or designedly to impoverish the subjects. The obligations of the law of nature cease not in society, but only in many cases are drawn closer, and have by human laws known penalties annexed to them to enforce their observation. Thus the law of nature stands as an eternal rule to all men, legislators as well as others. The rules that they make for other men's actions must, as well as their own and other men's actions, be conformable to the law of nature, *i.e.*, to the will of God, of which that is a declaration, and the fundamental law of nature being the preservation of mankind, no human sanction can be good or valid against it.

136. Secondly, The legislative, or supreme authority, cannot assume to itself a power to rule by extemporary arbitrary decrees, but is bound to dispense justice and decide the rights of the subject by promulgated standing laws,† and known authorized judges. For the law of nature

---

*"Two foundations there are which bear up public societies; the one a natural inclination whereby all men desire sociable life and fellowship; the other an order, expressly or secretly agreed upon, touching the manner of their union in living together. The latter is that which we call the law of a commonweal, the very soul of a politic body, the parts whereof are by law animated, held together, and set on work in such actions as the common good requireth. Laws politic, ordained for external order and regiment amongst men, are never framed as they should be, unless presuming the will of man to be inwardly obstinate, rebellious, and averse from all obedience to the sacred laws of his nature; in a word, unless presuming man to be in regard of his depraved mind little better than a wild beast, they do accordingly provide notwithstanding, so to frame his outward actions, that they be no hindrance unto the common good, for which societies are instituted. Unless they do this they are not perfect."—Hooker (*Eccl. Pol.*, lib. i, sect. 10).

†"Human laws are measures in respect of men whose actions they must direct, howbeit such measures they are as have also their higher rules to be measured by, which rules are two—the law of God and the law of nature; so that laws human must be made according to the general laws of nature, and without contradiction to any positive law of Scripture, otherwise they are ill made."—Hooker (*Eccl. Pol.*, lib. iii, sect. 9).

"To constrain men to anything inconvenient doth seem unreasonable."—(*ibid.*, lib. i, sect. 10).

being unwritten, and so nowhere to be found but in the minds of men, they who through passion or interest shall miscite or misapply it, cannot so easily be convinced of their mistake where there is no established judge. And so it serves not, as it ought, to determine the rights, and fence the properties of those that live under it, especially where every one is judge, interpreter, and executioner of it too, and that in his own case; and he that has right on his side, having ordinarily but his own single strength, hath not force enough to defend himself from injuries, or punish delinquents. To avoid these inconveniencies, which disorder men's properties in the state of nature, men unite into societies, that they may have the united strength of the whole society to secure and defend their properties, and may have standing rules to bound it, by which every one may know what is his. To this end it is that men give up all their natural power to the society which they enter into, and the community put the legislative power into such hands as they think fit, with this trust, that they shall be governed by declared laws, or else their peace, quiet, and property will still be at the same uncertainty as it was in the state of nature.

137. Absolute arbitrary power, or governing without settled standing laws, can neither of them consist with the ends of society and government, which men would not quit the freedom of the state of nature for, and tie themselves up under, were it not to preserve their lives, liberties, and fortunes; and by stated rules of right and property to secure their peace and quiet. It cannot be supposed that they should intend, had they a power so to do, to give to any one, or more, an absolute arbitrary power over their persons and estates, and put a force into the magistrate's hand to execute his unlimited will arbitrarily upon them. This were to put themselves into a worse condition than the state of nature, wherein they had a liberty to defend their right against the injuries of others, and were upon equal terms of force to maintain it, whether invaded by a single man or many in combination. Whereas, by supposing they have given up themselves to the absolute arbitrary power and will of a legislator, they have disarmed themselves, and armed him, to make prey of them when he pleases. He being in a much worse condition who is exposed to the arbitrary power of one man who has the command of 100,000, than he that is exposed to the arbitrary power of 100,000 single men; nobody being secure that his will, who hath such a command, is better than that of other men, though his force be 100,000 times stronger. And, therefore, whatever form the commonwealth is under, the ruling power ought to govern by declared and received laws, and not by extemporary dictates and undetermined resolutions. For then mankind will be in a far worse condition than in the state of nature, if they shall have armed one, or a few men, with the

joint power of a multitude to force them to obey at pleasure the exorbitant and unlimited decrees of their sudden thoughts, or unrestrained, and, till that moment, unknown wills, without having any measures set down which may guide and justify their actions. For all the power the government has, being only for the good of the society, as it ought not to be arbitrary and at pleasure, so it ought to be exercised by established and promulgated laws; that both the people may know their duty and be safe and secure within the limits of the law; and the rulers too kept within their due bounds, and not be tempted by the power they have in their hands to employ it to such purposes, and by such measures as they would not have known, and own not willingly.

138. Thirdly, The supreme power cannot take from any man any part of his property without his own consent. For the preservation of property being the end of government, and that for which men enter into society, it necessarily supposes and requires that the people should have property, without which they must be supposed to lose that, by entering into society, which was the end for which they entered into it; too gross an absurdity for any man to own. Men, therefore, in society having property, they have such a right to the goods which by the law of the community are theirs, that nobody hath a right to take their substance or any part of it[1] from them, without their own consent; without this they have no property at all. For I have truly no property in that which another can by right take from me when he pleases, against my consent. Hence it is a mistake to think that the supreme or legislative power of any commonwealth can do what it will, and dispose of the estates of the subjects arbitrarily, or take any part of them at pleasure. This is not much to be feared in governments where the legislative consists, wholly or in part, in assemblies which are variable, whose members, upon the dissolution of the assembly, are subjects under the common laws of their country, equally with the rest. But in governments where the legislative is in one lasting assembly, always in being, or in one man, as in absolute monarchies, there is danger still, that they will think themselves to have a distinct interest from the rest of the community, and so will be apt to increase their own riches and power by taking what they think fit from the people. For a man's property is not at all secure, though there be good and equitable laws to set the bounds of it between him and his fellow subjects, if he who commands those subjects have power to take from any private man what part he pleases of his property, and use and dispose of it as he thinks good.

139. But government, into whatsoever[2] hands it is put, being, as I

---

1. Altered in *errata* list in 3rd edition. Earlier editions read: "take them or any part of them from them, . . ."

2. Altered in 2nd edition. 1st edition reads: "whosesoever."

have before shewn, entrusted with this condition, and for this end, that men might have and secure their properties, the prince, or senate, however it may have power to make laws for the regulating of property between the subjects one amongst another, yet can never have a power to take to themselves the whole or any part of the subjects' property without their own consent. For this would be in effect to leave them no property at all. And to let us see that even absolute power, where it is necessary, is not arbitrary by being absolute, but is still limited by that reason, and confined to those ends, which required it in some cases to be absolute, we need look no farther than the common practice of martial discipline. For the preservation of the army, and in it of the whole commonwealth, requires an absolute obedience to the command of every superior officer, and it is justly death to disobey or dispute the most dangerous or unreasonable of them; but yet we see that neither the sergeant, that could command a soldier to march up to the mouth of a cannon, or stand in a breach, where he is almost sure to perish, can command that soldier to give him one penny of his money; nor the general, that can condemn him to death for deserting his post, or for not obeying the most desperate orders, can yet, with all his absolute power of life and death, dispose of one farthing of that soldier's estate, or seize one jot of his goods; whom yet he can command anything, and hang for the least disobedience. Because such a blind obedience is necessary to that end for which the commander has his power, *viz.*, the preservation of the rest; but the disposing of his goods has nothing to do with it.

140. 'Tis true governments cannot be supported without great charge, and 'tis fit every one who enjoys his share of the protection should pay out of his estate his proportion for the maintenance of it. But still it must be with his own consent, *i.e.*, the consent of the majority, giving it either by themselves or their representatives chosen by them. For if any one shall claim a power to lay and levy taxes on the people, by his own authority, and without such consent of the people, he thereby invades the fundamental law of property, and subverts the end of government. For what property have I in that which another may by right take when he pleases to himself?

141. Fourthly, The legislative cannot transfer the power of making laws to any other hands; for it being but a delegated power from the people, they who have it cannot pass it over to others. The people alone can appoint the form of the commonwealth, which is by constituting the legislative, and appointing in whose hands that shall be. And when the people have said, We will submit to rules,[3] and be governed by laws

---

3. "To rules" added in collected edition.

made by such men, and in such forms, nobody else can say other men shall make laws for them; nor can the people[4] be bound by any laws but such as are enacted by those whom they have chosen and authorized to make laws for them.

142. These are the bounds which the trust that is put in them by the society, and the law of God and nature, have set to the legislative power of every commonwealth, in all forms of government.

First, They are to govern by promulgated established laws, not to be varied in particular cases, but to have one rule for rich and poor, for the favourite at court and the countryman at plough.

Secondly, These laws also ought to be designed for no other end ultimately but the good of the people.

Thirdly, They must not raise taxes on the property of the people without the consent of the people, given by themselves or their deputies. And this properly concerns only such governments where the legislative is always in being, or at least where the people have not reserved any part of the legislative to deputies, to be from time to time chosen by themselves.

Fourthly, The legislative neither must nor can transfer the power of making laws to anybody else, or place it anywhere but where the people have.

Chapter XII

Of the Legislative, Executive, and Federative Power of the Commonwealth

143. The legislative power is that which has a right to direct how the force of the commonwealth shall be employed for preserving the community and the members of it. Because those laws which are constantly to be executed, and whose force is always to continue, may be made in a little time, therefore there is no need that the legislative should be always in being, not having always business to do. And because it may be too great a temptation to human frailty, apt to grasp at power, for the same persons, who have the power of making laws, to have also in their hands the power to execute them, whereby they may exempt themselves from obedience to the laws they make, and suit the law, both in its making and execution, to their own private advantage, and thereby come to have a distinct interest from the rest of the community, contrary to the end of society and government: therefore, in well ordered

---

4. "The people": collected edition. Earlier editions read: "they."

commonwealths, where the good of the whole is so considered as it ought, the legislative power is put into the hands of divers persons who, duly assembled, have by themselves or jointly with others a power to make laws, which when they have done, being separated again, they are themselves subject to the laws they have made; which is a new and near tie upon them, to take care that they make them for the public good.

144. But because the laws that are at once and in a short time made, have a constant and lasting force and need a perpetual execution or an attendance thereunto; therefore 'tis necessary there should be a power always in being, which should see to the execution of the laws that are made and remain in force; and thus the legislative and executive power come often to be separated.

145. There is another power in every commonwealth, which one may call natural, because it is that which answers to the power every man naturally had before he entered into society; for though in a commonwealth the members of it are distinct persons still in reference to one another, and as such are governed by the laws of the society, yet in reference to the rest of mankind they make one body, which is, as every member of it before was, still in the state of nature with the rest of mankind. Hence it is[1] that the controversies that happen between any man of the society with those that are out of it are managed by the public, and an injury done to a member of their body engages the whole in the reparation of it. So that under this consideration the whole community is one body in the state of nature in respect of all other states or persons out of its community.

146. This therefore contains the power of war and peace, leagues and alliances, and all the transactions with all persons and communities without the commonwealth, and may be called federative if any one pleases. So the thing be understood, I am indifferent as to the name.

147. These two powers, executive and federative, though they be really distinct in themselves, yet one comprehending the execution of the municipal laws of the society within itself upon all that are parts of it; the other the management of the security and interest of the public without, with all those that it may receive benefit or damage from, yet they are always almost united. And though this federative power in the well or ill management of it be of great moment to the commonwealth, yet it is much less capable to be directed by antecedent, standing, positive laws than the executive; and so must necessarily be left to the prudence and wisdom of those whose hands it is in, to be managed for the

---

1. 2nd edition. 1st edition reads: "So that the controversies . . ."

public good. For the laws that concern subjects one amongst another, being to direct their actions, may well enough precede them. But what is to be done in reference to foreigners, depending much upon their actions and the variation of designs and interests, must be left in great part to the prudence of those who have this power committed to them, to be managed by the best of their skill for the advantage of the commonwealth.

148. Though, as I said, the executive and federative power of every community be really distinct in themselves, yet they are hardly to be separated and placed at the same time in the hands of distinct persons; for both of them requiring the force of the society for their exercise, it is almost impracticable to place the force of the commonwealth in distinct and not subordinate hands; or that the executive and federative power should be placed in persons that might act separately, whereby the force of the public would be under different commands, which would be apt some time or other to cause disorder and ruin.

Chapter XIII

Of the Subordination of the Powers of the Commonwealth

149. Though in a constituted commonwealth, standing upon its own basis, and acting according to its own nature, that is, acting for the preservation of the community, there can be but one supreme power, which is the legislative, to which all the rest are and must be subordinate, yet the legislative being only a fiduciary power to act for certain ends, there remains still in the people a supreme power to remove or alter the legislative, when they find the legislative act contrary to the trust reposed in them; for all power given with trust for the attaining an end being limited by that end, whenever that end is manifestly neglected or opposed, the trust must necessarily be forfeited, and the power devolve into the hands of those that gave it, who may place it anew where they shall think best for their safety and security. And thus the community perpetually retains a supreme power of saving themselves from the attempts and designs of any body, even of their legislators, whenever they shall be so foolish or so wicked as to lay and carry on designs against the liberties and properties of the subject; for no man or society of men, having a power to deliver up their preservation, or consequently the means of it, to the absolute will and arbitrary dominion of another, whenever any one shall go about to bring them into such a slavish condition, they will always have a right to preserve what they have not a power to part with; and to rid themselves of those who

invade this fundamental, sacred, and unalterable law of self-preservation for which they entered into society. And thus the community may be said in this respect to be always the supreme power, but not as considered under any form of government, because this power of the people can never take place till the government be dissolved.

150. In all cases, whilst the government subsists, the legislative is the supreme power; for what can give laws to another must needs be superior to him, and since the legislative is no otherwise legislative of the society but by the right it has to make laws for all the parts and for every member of the society, prescribing rules to their actions, and giving power of execution where they are transgressed, the legislative must needs be the supreme, and all other powers in any members or parts of the society derived from and subordinate to it.

151. In some commonwealths, where the legislative is not always in being, and the executive is vested in a single person, who has also a share in the legislative, there that single person in a very tolerable sense may also be called supreme: not that he has in himself all the supreme power, which is that of law-making, but because he has in him the supreme execution, from whom all inferior magistrates derive all their several subordinate powers, or at least the greatest part of them; having also no legislative superior to him, there being no law to be made without his consent, which cannot be expected should ever subject him to the other part of the legislative, he is properly enough in this sense supreme. But yet it is to be observed, that though oaths of allegiance and fealty are taken to him, it is not to him as supreme legislator, but as supreme executor of the law, made by a joint power of him with others; allegiance being nothing but an obedience according to law, which when he violates, he has no right to obedience, nor can claim it otherwise than as the public person vested with the power of the law, and so is to be considered as the image, phantom, or representative of the commonwealth, acted by the will of the society, declared in its laws; and thus he has no will, no power, but that of the law. But when he quits this representation, this public will, and acts by his own private will, he degrades himself, and is but a single private person without power, and without will that has any right to obedience[1]; the members owing no obedience but to the public will of the society.

152. The executive power, placed anywhere but in a person that has also a share in the legislative, is visibly subordinate and accountable to it, and may be at pleasure changed and displaced; so that it is not the supreme executive power that is exempt from subordination, but the supreme executive power vested in one, who, having a share in the leg-

---

1. "That has any right to obedience" added in 2nd edition.

islative, has no distinct superior legislative to be subordinate and accountable to, farther than he himself shall join and consent; so that he
is no more subordinate than he himself shall think fit, which one may
certainly conclude will be but very little. Of other ministerial and subordinate powers in a commonwealth we need not speak, they being so
multiplied with infinite variety, in the different customs and constitutions of distinct commonwealths, that it is impossible to give a particular account of them all. Only thus much, which is necessary to our
present purpose, we may take notice of concerning them, that they
have no manner of authority, any of them, beyond what is by positive
grant and commission delegated to them, and are all of them accountable to some other power in the commonwealth.

153. It is not necessary, no nor so much as convenient, that the legislative should be always in being; but absolutely necessary that the executive power should, because there is not always need of new laws to
be made, but always need of execution of the laws that are made. When
the legislative hath put the execution of the laws they make into other
hands, they have a power still to resume it out of those hands when they
find cause, and to punish for any mal-administration against the laws.
The same holds also in regard of the federative power, that and the executive being both ministerial and subordinate to the legislative,
which, as has been shewn, in a constituted commonwealth is the
supreme. The legislative also in this case being supposed to consist of
several persons (for if it be a single person, it cannot but be always in
being, and so will, as supreme, naturally have the supreme executive
power, together with the legislative), may assemble and exercise their
legislature[2] at the times that either their original constitution or their
own adjournment appoints, or when they please; if neither of these
hath appointed any time, or there be no other way prescribed to con-
voke them. For the supreme power being placed in them by the people, 'tis always in them, and they may exercise it when they please,
unless by their original constitution they are limited to certain seasons, or
by an act of their supreme power they have adjourned to a certain time;
and when that time comes they have a right to assemble and act again.

154. If the legislative or any part of it be made up[3] of representatives
chosen for that time by the people, which afterwards return into the ordinary state of subjects, and have no share in the legislature but upon
a new choice, this power of choosing must also be exercised by the
people, either at certain appointed seasons, or else when they are sum-
moned to it; and in this latter case the power of convoking the legisla-

---

2. Altered in collected edition. Earlier editions read: "legislative."
3. "Made up" added in *errata* list in 3rd edition.

tive is ordinarily placed in the executive, and has one of these two limitations in respect of time: that either the original constitution requires their assembling and acting at certain intervals, and then the executive power does nothing but ministerially issue directions for their electing and assembling, according to due forms; or else it is left to his prudence to call them by new elections when the occasions or exigencies of the public require the amendment of old, or making of new laws, or the redress or prevention of any inconveniencies that lie on or threaten the people.

155. It may be demanded here, What if the executive power, being possessed of the force of the commonwealth, shall make use of that force to hinder the meeting and acting of the legislative, when the original constitution or the public exigencies require it? I say using force upon the people without authority, and contrary to the trust put in him that does so, is a state of war with the people, who have a right to reinstate their legislative in the exercise of their power. For having erected a legislative, with an intent they should exercise the power of making laws, either at certain set times, or when there is need of it, when they are hindered by any force from what is so necessary to the society, and wherein the safety and preservation of the people consists, the people have a right to remove it by force. In all states and conditions the true remedy of force without authority is to oppose force to it. The use of force without authority always puts him that uses it into a state of war, as the aggressor, and renders him liable to be treated accordingly.

156. The power of assembling and dismissing the legislative, placed in the executive, gives not the executive a superiority over it, but is fiduciary trust placed in him, for the safety of the people in a case where the uncertainty and variableness of human affairs could not bear a steady fixed rule. For it not being possible that the first framers of the government should, by any foresight, be so much masters of future events as to be able to prefix so just periods of return and duration to the assemblies of the legislative in all times to come, that might exactly answer all the exigencies of the commonwealth, the best remedy could be found for this defect was to trust this to the prudence of one who was always to be present, and whose business it was to watch over the public good. Constant frequent meetings of the legislative, and long continuations of their assemblies, without necessary occasion, could not but be burdensome to the people, and must necessarily in time produce more dangerous inconveniencies, and yet the quick turn of affairs might be sometimes such as to need their present help. Any delay of their convening might endanger the public; and sometimes too their business might be so great that the limited time of their sitting might be too short for their work, and rob the public of that ben-

efit which could be had only from their mature deliberation. What then could be done in this case to prevent the community from being exposed some time or other to imminent hazard on one side or the other, by fixed intervals and periods set to the meeting and acting of the legislative, but to entrust it to the prudence of some, who being present, and acquainted with the state of public affairs, might make use of this prerogative for the public good? And where else could this be so well placed as in his hands, who was entrusted with the execution of the laws for the same end? Thus, supposing the regulation of times for the assembling and sitting of the legislative not settled by the original constitution, it naturally fell into the hands of the executive, not as an arbitrary power depending on his good pleasure, but with this trust always to have it exercised only for the public weal, as the occurrences of times and change of affairs might require. Whether settled periods of their convening, or a liberty left to the prince for convoking the legislative, or perhaps a mixture of both, hath the least inconvenience attending it, it is not my business here to inquire, but only to shew, that though the executive power may have the prerogative of convoking and dissolving such conventions of the legislative, yet it is not thereby superior to it.

157. Things of this world are in so constant a flux that nothing remains long in the same state. Thus people, riches, trade, power, change their stations, flourishing mighty cities come to ruin, and prove in time neglected, desolate corners, whilst other unfrequented places grow into populous countries, filled with wealth and inhabitants. But things not always changing equally, and private interest often keeping up customs and privileges when the reasons of them are ceased, it often comes to pass that in governments where part of the legislative consists of representatives chosen by the people, that in tract of time this representation becomes very unequal and disproportionate to the reasons it was first established upon. To what gross absurdities the following of custom, when reason has left it, may lead, we may be satisfied, when we see the bare name of a town, of which there remains not so much as the ruins, where scarce so much housing as a sheepcote, or more inhabitants than a shepherd is to be found, sends as many representatives to the grand assembly of law-makers as a whole county numerous in people and powerful in riches. This strangers stand amazed at, and every one must confess needs a remedy; though most think it hard to find one, because the constitution of the legislative being the original and supreme act of the society, antecedent to all positive laws in it, and depending wholly on the people, no inferior power can alter it. And therefore the people, when the legislative is once constituted, having in such a government as we have been speaking of no power to act as long

as the government stands, this inconvenience is thought incapable of a remedy.

158. *Salus populi suprema lex* is certainly so just and fundamental a rule that he who sincerely follows it cannot dangerously err. If therefore the executive, who has the power of convoking the legislative, observing rather the true proportion than fashion of representation, regulates, not by old custom, but true reason, the number of members in all places that have a right to be distinctly represented, which no part of the people however incorporated can pretend to, but in proportion to the assistance which it affords to the public, it cannot be judged to have set up a new legislative, but to have restored the old and true one, and to have rectified the disorders which succession of time had insensibly as well as inevitably introduced. For it being the interest as well as intention of the people, to have a fair and equal representative, whosoever brings it nearest to that is an undoubted friend to and establisher of the government, and cannot miss the consent and approbation of the community; prerogative being nothing but a power in the hands of the prince to provide for the public good in such cases which, depending upon unforeseen and uncertain occurrences, certain and unalterable laws could not safely direct. Whatsoever shall be done manifestly for the good of the people, and the establishing the government upon its true foundations is, and always will be, just prerogative. The power of erecting new corporations, and therewith new representatives, carries with it a supposition that in time the measures of representation might vary, and those places[4] have a just right to be represented which before had none; and by the same reason those cease to have a right, and be too inconsiderable for such a privilege which before had it. 'Tis not a change from the present state, which perhaps corruption or decay has introduced, that makes an inroad upon the government, but the tendency of it to injure or oppress the people, and to set up one part or party with a distinction from and an unequal subjection of the rest. Whatsoever cannot but be acknowledged to be of advantage to the society and people in general upon just and lasting measures, will always, when done, justify itself; and whenever the people shall choose their representatives upon just and undeniably equal measures, suitable to the original frame of the government, it cannot be doubted to be the will and act of the society who ever permitted or caused[5] them so to do.

---

4. "Places" added in *errata* list in 3rd edition.
5. Collected edition. Earlier editions read: "proposed to them . . ."

Chapter XIV

Of Prerogative

159. Where the legislative and executive power are in distinct hands (as they are in all moderated monarchies and well-framed governments) there the good of the society requires that several things should be left to the discretion of him that has the executive power. For the legislators not being able to foresee and provide by laws for all that may be useful to the community, the executor of the laws, having the power in his hands, has by the common law of nature a right to make use of it for the good of the society, in many cases, where the municipal law has given no direction, till the legislative can conveniently be assembled to provide for it. Many things there are which the law can by no means provide for, and those must necessarily be left to the discretion of him that has the executive power in his hands, to be ordered by him as the public good and advantage shall require. Nay, it is fit that the laws themselves should in some case give way to the executive power, or rather to this fundamental law of nature and government, *viz.*, that as much as may be all the members of the society are to be preserved. For since many accidents may happen wherein a strict and rigid observation of the laws may do harm (as not to pull down an innocent man's house to stop the fire when the next to it is burning), and a man may come sometimes within the reach of the law, which makes no distinction of persons by an action that may deserve reward and pardon, 'tis fit the ruler should have a power in many cases to mitigate the severity of the law, and pardon some offenders: for the end of government being the preservation of all, as much as may be, even the guilty are to be spared where it can prove no prejudice to the innocent.

160. This power to act according to discretion for the public good, without the prescription of the law, and sometimes even against it, is that which is called prerogative. For since in some governments the law-making power is not always in being, and is usually too numerous, and so too slow, for the dispatch requisite to execution; and because also it is impossible to foresee, and so by laws to provide for, all accidents and necessities that may concern the public, or to make such laws as will do no harm if they are executed with an inflexible rigour on all occasions and upon all persons that may come in their way; therefore there is a latitude left to the executive power to do many things of choice which the laws do not prescribe.

161. This power, whilst employed for the benefit of the community, and suitably to the trust and ends of the government, is undoubted prerogative, and never is questioned. For the people are very seldom or

never scrupulous or nice in the point; they are far from examining[1] prerogative whilst it is in any tolerable degree employed for the use it was meant, that is for the good of the people, and not manifestly against it. But if there comes to be a question between the executive power and the people about a thing claimed as a prerogative, the tendency of the exercise of such prerogative to the good or hurt of the people will easily decide that question.

162. It is easy to conceive that in the infancy of governments, when commonwealths differed little from families in number of people, they differed from them too but little in number of laws; and the governors, being as the fathers of them, watching over them for their good, the government was almost all prerogative. A few established laws served the turn, and the discretion and care of the ruler supplied the rest. But when mistake or flattery prevailed with weak princes to make use of this power for private ends of their own, and not for the public good, the people were fain by express laws to get prerogative determined in those points wherein they found disadvantage from it, and thus declared limitations of prerogative were by the people found necessary in cases[2] which they and their ancestors had left, in the utmost latitude, to the wisdom of those princes, who made no other but a right use of it, that is for the good of the people.

163. And therefore they have a very wrong notion of government who say that the people have encroached upon the prerogative when they have got any part of it to be defined by positive laws. For in so doing they have not pulled from the prince anything that of right belonged to him, but only declared that that power which they indefinitely left in his or his ancestors' hands, to be exercised for their good, was not a thing which they intended him when he used it otherwise. For the end of government being the good of the community, whatsoever alterations are made in it tending to that end, cannot be an encroachment upon any body, since no body in government can have a right tending to any other end. And those only are encroachments which prejudice or hinder the public good. Those who say otherwise speak as if the prince had a distinct and separate interest from the good of the community, and was not made for it; the root and source from which spring almost all those evils and disorders which happen in kingly governments. And indeed if that be so, the people under his government are not a society of rational creatures entered into a community for their mutual good; they are not[3] such as have set rulers over

---

1. Altered in 2nd edition. 1st edition reads: ". . . point, or questioning of prerogative . . ."
2. Altered in collected edition. Earlier editions read: ". . . prerogative in those cases which . . ."
3. The words "they are not" were added in the 2nd edition.

themselves to guard and promote that good, but are to be looked on as a herd of inferior creatures under the dominion of a master, who keeps them and works them for his own pleasure or profit. If men were so void of reason and brutish as to enter into society on such terms, prerogative might indeed be, what some men would have it, an arbitrary power to do things hurtful to the people.

164. But since a rational creature cannot be supposed, when free, to put himself into subjection to another for his own harm (though where he finds a good and a wise ruler, he may not perhaps think it either necessary or useful to set precise bounds to his power in all things), prerogative can be nothing but the people's permitting their rulers to do several things of their own free choice where the law was silent, and sometimes, too, against the direct letter of the law, for the public good, and their acquiescing in it when so done; for as a good prince, who is mindful of the trust put into his hands, and careful of the good of his people, cannot have too much prerogative, that is, power to do good, so a weak and ill prince, who would claim that power which his predecessors exercised, without the direction of the law as a prerogative belonging to him by right of his office, which he may exercise at his pleasure, to make or promote an interest distinct from that of the public, gives the people an occasion to claim their right and limit that power, which, whilst it was exercised for their good, they were content should be tacitly allowed.

165. And, therefore, he that will look into the history of England will find that prerogative was always largest in the hands of our wisest and best princes, because the people, observing the whole tendency of their actions to be the public good, contested not what was done without law to that end,[4] or if any human frailty or mistake (for princes are but men, made as others) appeared in some small declinations from that end, yet 'twas visible the main of their conduct tended to nothing but the care of the public. The people, therefore, finding reason to be satisfied with these princes whenever they acted without or contrary to the letter of the law, acquiesced in what they did, and, without the least complaint, let them enlarge their prerogative as they pleased, judging rightly that they did nothing herein to the prejudice of their laws, since they acted conformable to the foundation and end of all laws, the public good.

166. Such god-like princes, indeed, had some title to arbitrary power by that argument that would prove absolute monarchy the best government, as that which God himself governs the universe by, because such kings partake of his wisdom and goodness. Upon this is founded that saying, that the reigns of good princes have always been most dan-

---

4. The words "contested not . . . to that end" were added in the collected edition.

gerous to the liberties of their people; for when their successors, managing the government with different thoughts, would draw the actions of those good rulers into precedent, and make them the standard of their prerogative, as if what had been done only for the good of the people was a right in them to do for the harm of the people if they so pleased, it has often occasioned contest, and sometimes public disorders, before the people could recover their original right, and get that to be declared not to be prerogative, which truly was never so, since it is impossible that anybody in the society should ever have a right to do the people harm; though it be very possible and reasonable that the people should not go about to set any bounds to the prerogative of those kings or rulers who themselves transgressed not the bounds of the public good; for prerogative is nothing but the power of doing public good without a rule.

167. The power of calling parliaments in England, as to precise time, place, and duration, is certainly a prerogative of the king, but still with this trust, that it shall be made use of for the good of the nation as the exigencies of the times and variety of occasions shall require; for it being impossible to foresee which should always be the fittest place for them to assemble in, and what the best season, the choice of these was left with the executive power, as might be most[5] subservient to the public good, and best suit the ends of parliaments.

168. The old question will be asked in this matter of prerogative: But who shall be judge when this power is made a right use of? I answer: Between an executive power in being, with such a prerogative, and a legislative that depends upon his will for their convening, there can be no judge on earth; as there can be none between the legislative and the people, should either the executive or the legislative, when they have got the power in their hands, design or go about to enslave or destroy them. The people have no other remedy in this, as in all other cases where they have no judge on earth, but to appeal to heaven; for the rulers in such attempts, exercising a power the people never put into their hands (who can never be supposed to consent that anybody should rule over them for their harm) do that which they have not a right to do. And where the body of the people, or any single man, is deprived of their right, or is under the exercise of a power without right, and have no appeal on earth, there they have a liberty to appeal to heaven, whenever they judge the cause of sufficient moment. And, therefore, though the people cannot be judge so as to have by the constitution of that society any superior power, to determine and give effective sentence in the case, yet they have, by a law antecedent and

---

5. Altered from "best" in *errata* list in 2nd edition.

paramount to all positive laws of men, reserved that ultimate determination to themselves which belongs to all mankind, where there lies no appeal on earth, *viz.*, to judge[6] whether they have just cause to make their appeal to heaven. And this judgment they cannot part with, it being out of man's power so to submit himself to another as to give him a liberty to destroy him, God and nature never allowing a man so to abandon himself as to neglect his own preservation; and, since he cannot take away his own life, neither can he give another power to take it. Nor let any one think this lays a perpetual foundation for disorder, for this operates not till the inconveniency is so great that the majority feel it and are weary of it, and find a necessity to have it amended. But this the executive power or wise princes never need come in the danger of, and it is the thing of all others they have most need to avoid, as of all others the most perilous.

Chapter XV

Of Paternal, Political, and Despotical Power Considered Together

169. Though I have had occasion to speak of these separately before, yet the great mistakes of late about government having, as I suppose, arisen from confounding these distinct powers one with another, it may not, perhaps, be amiss to consider them here together.

170. First, then, Paternal or parental power is nothing but that which parents have over their children, to govern them for their children's good, till they come to the use of reason or a state of knowledge, wherein they may be supposed capable to understand that rule, whether it be the law of nature or the municipal law of their country, they are to govern themselves by—capable, I say, to know it as well as several others who live as freemen under that law. The affection and tenderness which God hath planted in the breasts of parents towards their children makes it evident that this is not intended to be a severe arbitrary government, but only for the help, instruction, and preservation of their offspring. But, happen it as it will, there is, as I have proved, no reason why it should be thought to extend to life and death at any time over their children more than over anybody else; neither can there be any pretence why this parental power should keep the

---

6. Altered in collected edition. Earlier editions read: ". . . they have reserved that ultimate determination to themselves which belongs to all mankind, where there lies no appeal on earth, by a law antecedent and paramount to all positive laws of men, whether they have just cause . . ."

child, when grown to a man, in subjection to the will of his parents,[1] any farther than as having received life and education from his parents obliges him to respect, honour, gratitude, assistance and support, all his life, to both father and mother. And thus, 'tis true, the paternal is a natural government, but not all extending itself to the ends and jurisdictions of that which is political. The power of the father does not reach at all to the property of the child, which is only in his own disposing.

171. Secondly, Political power is that power which every man having in the state of nature has given up into the hands of the society, and therein to the governors whom the society hath set over itself, with this express or tacit trust, that it shall be employed for their good and the preservation of their property. Now this power, which every man has in the state of nature, and which he parts with to the society in all such cases where the society can secure him, is to use such means for the preserving of his own property as he thinks good and nature allows him, and to punish the breach of the law of nature in others so as (according to the best of his reason) may most conduce to the preservation of himself and the rest of mankind. So that the end and measure of this power, when in every man's hands in the state of nature, being the preservation of all of his society—that is, all mankind in general—it can have no other end or measure, when in the hands of the magistrates, but to preserve the members of that society in their lives, liberties, and possessions; and so cannot be an absolute, arbitrary power over their lives and fortunes, which are as much as possible to be preserved, but a power to make laws, and annex such penalties to them, as may tend to the preservation of the whole, by cutting off those parts, and those only, which are so corrupt that they threaten the sound and healthy, without which no severity is lawful. And this power has its original only from compact and agreement, and the mutual consent of those who make up the community.

172. Thirdly, Despotical power is an absolute, arbitrary power one man has over another to take away his life whenever he pleases. This is a power which neither nature gives, for it has made no such distinction between one man and another, nor compact can convey; for man, not having such an arbitrary power over his own life, cannot give another man such a power over it; but it is the effect only of forfeiture, which the aggressor makes of his own life, when he puts himself into the state of war with another. For having quitted reason, which God hath given to be the rule betwixt man and man, and the common bond, whereby

1. Altered in collected edition. Earlier editions read: ". . . anybody else; or keep the child in subjection to the will of his parents when grown to a man and the perfect use of reason, any farther . . ."

human kind is united into one fellowship and society; and having renounced the way of peace, which that teaches, and made use of the force of war, to compass his unjust ends upon another, where he has no right; and so revolting from his own kind to that of beasts, by making force, which is theirs, to be his rule of right, he renders himself liable to be destroyed by the injured person, and the rest of mankind that will join with him in the execution of justice, as any other wild beast or noxious brute, with whom mankind can have neither society nor security.[2] And thus captives, taken in a just and lawful war, and such only, are subject to a despotical power, which, as it arises not from compact, so neither is it capable of any, but is the state of war continued. For what compact can be made with a man that is not master of his own life? What condition can he perform? And if he be once allowed to be master of his own life, the despotical, arbitrary power of his master ceases. He that is master of himself and his own life has a right too to the means of preserving it; so that as soon as compact enters slavery ceases, and he so far quits his absolute power, and puts an end to the state of war, who enters into conditions with his captive.

173. Nature gives the first of these, *viz.* paternal power to parents for the benefit of their children during their minority, to supply their want of ability, and understanding how to manage their property. (By property I must be understood here, as in other places, to mean that property which men have in their persons as well as goods.) Voluntary agreement gives the second, *viz.* political power to governors for the benefit of their subjects, to secure them in the possession and use of their properties. And forfeiture gives the third despotical power to lords for their own benefit, over those who are stripped of all property.

174. He that shall consider the distinct rise and extent, and the different ends of these several powers, will plainly see that paternal power comes as far short of that of the magistrate as despotical exceeds it; and that absolute dominion, however placed, is so far from being one kind of civil society that it is as inconsistent with it as slavery is with property. Paternal power is only where minority makes the child incapable to manage his property; political where men have property in their own disposal; and despotical over such as have no property at all.

2. Altered in collected edition. Earlier editions read: ". . . betwixt man and man, and the peaceable ways which that teaches, and made use of force to compass his unjust ends upon another, where he has no right, he renders himself liable to be destroyed by his adversary, whenever he can, as any other noxious and brutish creature that is destructive to his being. And thus . . ." A footnote in the 6th edition states that "another copy corrected by Mr. Locke has it thus: *Noxious brute that is destructive to their being*." This version in fact appears in a MS. note in the Christ's College copy of the 3rd edition, stating "C'est ainsi que Mr. L. a corrigé cet endroit dans l'exemplaire par lequel il souhaite que son livre soit rimprimé après sa mort."

Chapter XVI

Of Conquest

175. Though governments can originally have no other rise than that before-mentioned, nor polities be founded on anything but the consent of the people, yet such has been the disorders ambition has filled the world with, that, in the noise of war, which makes so great a part of the history of mankind, this consent is little taken notice of; and therefore many have mistaken the force of arms for the consent of the people, and reckon conquest as one of the originals of government. But conquest is as far from setting up any government as demolishing a house is from building a new one in the place. Indeed, it often makes way for a new frame of a commonwealth, by destroying the former; but, without consent of the people, can never erect a new one.

176. That the aggressor, who puts himself into the state of war with another, and unjustly invades another man's right, can by such an unjust war never come to have a right over the conquered, will be easily agreed by all men, who will not think that robbers and pirates have a right of empire over whomsoever they have force enough to master, or that men are bound by promises which unlawful force extorts from them. Should a robber break into my house, and, with a dagger at my throat, make me seal deeds to convey my estate to him, would this give him any title? Just such a title by his sword has an unjust conqueror who forces me into submission. The injury and the crime is equal, whether committed by the wearer of a crown or some petty villain. The title of the offender and the number of his followers make no difference in the offence, unless it be to aggravate it. The only difference is, great robbers punish little ones to keep them in their obedience; but the great ones are rewarded with laurels and triumphs, because they are too big for the weak hands of justice in this world, and have the power in their own possession, which should punish offenders. What is my remedy against a robber that so broke into my house? Appeal to the law for justice. But perhaps justice is denied, or I am crippled and cannot stir, robbed and have not the means to do it. If God has taken away all means of seeking remedy, there is nothing left but patience. But my son, when able, may seek the relief of the law, which I am denied; he or his son may renew his appeal, till he recover his right. But the conquered, or their children, have no court, no arbitrator on earth to appeal to. Then they may appeal, as Jephtha did, to heaven, and repeat their appeal, till they recovered the native right of their ancestors, which was to have such a legislative over them as the majority should approve and freely acquiesce in. If it be objected, This would cause

endless trouble; I answer, no more than justice does, where she lies open to all that appeal to her. He that troubles his neighbour without a cause is punished for it by the justice of the court he appeals to. And he that appeals to heaven must be sure he has right on his side; and a right, too, that is worth the trouble and cost of his appeal, as he will answer at a tribunal that cannot be deceived, and will be sure to retribute to every one according to the mischiefs he hath created to his fellow-subjects, that is, any part of mankind. From whence 'tis plain that he that conquers in an unjust war can thereby have no title to the subjection and obedience of the conquered.

177. But supposing victory favours the right side, let us consider a conqueror in a lawful war, and see what power he gets, and over whom.

First, 'Tis plain he gets no power by his conquest over those that conquered with him. They that fought on his side cannot suffer by the conquest, but must, at least, be as much freemen as they were before. And most commonly they serve upon terms, and on condition to share with their leader, and enjoy a part of the spoil, and other advantages that attend the conquering sword; or, at least, have a part of the subdued country bestowed upon them. And the conquering people are not, I hope, to be slaves by conquest, and wear their laurels only to show they are sacrifices to their leader's triumph. They that found absolute monarchy upon the title of the sword make their heroes, who are the founders of such monarchies, arrant Draw-can-sirs, and forget they had any officers and soldiers that fought on their side in the battles they won, or assisted them in the subduing, or shared in possessing, the countries they mastered. We are told by some that the English monarchy is founded in the Norman conquest, and that our princes have thereby a title to absolute dominion; which, if it were true (as by history it appears otherwise), and that William had a right to make war on this island, yet his dominion by conquest could reach no farther than to the Saxons and Britons that were then inhabitants of this country. The Normans that came with him, and helped to conquer, and all descended from them, are freemen, and no subjects by conquest; let that give what dominion it will. And if I, or anybody else, shall claim freedom, as derived from them, it will be very hard to prove the contrary. And 'tis plain, the law that has made no distinction between the one and the other, intends not there should be any difference in their freedom or privileges.

178. But supposing, which seldom happens, that the conquerors and conquered never incorporate into one people, under the same laws and freedom. Let us see next what power a lawful conqueror has over the subdued: and that I say is purely despotical. He has an absolute power over the lives of those who by an unjust war have forfeited them; but

not over the lives or fortunes of those who engaged not in the war, nor over the possessions even of those who were actually engaged in it.

179. Secondly, I say then the conqueror gets no power but only over those who have actually assisted, concurred, or consented to that unjust force that is used against him. For the people having given to their governors no power to do an unjust thing, such as is to make an unjust war (for they never had such a power in themselves), they ought not to be charged as guilty of the violence and injustice that is committed in an unjust war, any farther than they actually abet it; no more than they are to be thought guilty of any violence or oppression their governors should use upon the people themselves, or any part of their fellow-subjects, they having empowered them no more to the one than to the other. Conquerors, 'tis true, seldom trouble themselves to make the distinction, but they willingly permit the confusion of war to sweep all together; but yet this alters not the right, for the conqueror's power over the lives of the conquered, being only because they have used force to do or maintain an injustice, he can have the power only over those who have concurred in that force; all the rest are innocent; and he has no more title over the people of that country, who have done him no injury, and so have made no forfeiture of their lives, than he has over any other, who without any injuries or provocations have lived upon fair terms with him.

180. Thirdly, The power a conqueror gets over those he overcomes in a just war, is perfectly despotical; he has an absolute power over the lives of those who, by putting themselves in a state of war, have forfeited them; but he has not thereby a right and title to their possessions. This I doubt not but at first sight will seem a strange doctrine, it being so quite contrary to the practice of the world; there being nothing more familiar in speaking of the dominion of countries, than to say such an one conquered it; as if conquest, without any more ado, conveyed a right of possession. But when we consider, that the practice of the strong and powerful, how universal soever it may be, is seldom the rule of right, however it be one part of the subjection of the conquered, not to argue against the conditions cut out to them by the conquering sword.

181. Though in all war there be usually a complication of force and damage, and the aggressor seldom fails to harm the estate, when he uses force against the persons of those he makes war upon, yet 'tis the use of force only that puts a man into the state of war. For whether by force he begins the injury, or else having quietly, and by fraud, done the injury, he refuses to make reparation, and by force maintains it (which is the same thing, as at first to have done it by force), 'tis the unjust use of force that makes the war. For he that breaks open my house,

and violently turns me out of doors, or having peaceably got in, by force keeps me out, does in effect the same thing; supposing we are in such a state, that we have no common judge on earth whom I may appeal to, and to whom we are both obliged to submit, for of such I am now speaking. 'Tis the unjust use of force, then, that puts a man into the state of war with another, and thereby he that is guilty of it makes a forfeiture of his life. For quitting reason, which is the rule given between man and man, and using force, the way of beasts, he becomes liable to be destroyed by him he uses force against, as any savage ravenous beast that is dangerous to his being.

182. But because the miscarriages of the father are no faults of the children, and they may be rational and peaceable, notwithstanding the brutishness and injustice of the father; the father, by his miscarriages and violence, can forfeit but his own life, but involves not his children in his guilt or destruction. His goods, which nature, that willeth the preservation of all mankind as much as is possible, hath made to belong to the children to keep them from perishing, do still continue to belong to his children. For supposing them not to have joined in the war, either through infancy, absence[1] or choice, they have done nothing to forfeit them; nor has the conqueror any right to take them away, by the bare title[2] of having subdued him that by force attempted his destruction; though perhaps he may have some right to them, to repair the damages he has sustained by the war, and the defence of his own right; which how far it reaches to the possessions of the conquered we shall see by-and-by. So that he that by conquest has a right over a man's person to destroy him if he pleases, has not thereby a right over his estate to possess and enjoy it. For it is the brutal force the aggressor has used that gives his adversary a right to take away his life, and destroy him if he pleases, as a noxious creature, but 'tis damage sustained that alone gives him title to another man's goods. For though I may kill a thief that sets on me in the highway, yet I may not (which seems less) take away his money, and let him go; this would be robbery on my side. His force, and the state of war he put himself in, made him forfeit his life, but gave me no title to his goods. The right then of conquest extends only to the lives of those who joined in the war, not to their estates, but only in order to make reparation for the damages received, and the charges of the war, and that too with reservation of the right of the innocent wife and children.

183. Let the conqueror have as much justice on his side as could be supposed, he has no right to seize more than the vanquished could for-

---

1. "Absence" added in collected edition.
2. "Title" in collected edition. Earlier editions read: "right."

feit; his life is at the victor's mercy, and his service, and goods he may appropriate, to make himself reparation, but he cannot take the goods of his wife and children; they too had a title to the goods he enjoyed, and their shares in the estate he possessed. For example, I in the state of nature (and all commonwealths are in the state of nature one with another) have injured another man, and refusing to give satisfaction, it comes to a state of war, wherein my defending by force what I had gotten unjustly, makes me the aggressor. I am conquered: my life, 'tis true, as forfeit, is at mercy, but not my wife's and children's. They made not the war, nor assisted in it. I could not forfeit their lives; they were not mine to forfeit. My wife had a share in my estate; that neither could I forfeit. And my children also, being born of me, had a right to be maintained out of my labour or substance. Here then is the case: the conqueror has a title to reparation for damages received, and the children have a title to their father's estate for their subsistence. For as to the wife's share, whether her own labour or compact gave her a title to it, 'tis plain her husband could not forfeit what was hers. What must be done in the case? I answer: The fundamental law of nature being, that all, as much as may be, should be preserved, it follows, that if there be not enough fully to satisfy both, *viz.*, for the conqueror's losses, and children's maintenance, he that hath and to spare must remit something of his full satisfaction, and give way to the pressing and preferable title of those who are in danger to perish without it.

184. But supposing the charge and damages of the war are to be made up to the conqueror to the utmost farthing; and that the children of the vanquished, spoiled of all their father's goods, are to be left to starve and perish; yet the satisfying of what shall, on this score, be due to the conqueror, will scarce give him a title to any country he shall conquer. For the damages of war can scarce amount to the value of any considerable tract of land, in any part of the world, where all the land is possessed, and none lies waste. And if I have not taken away the conqueror's land, which, being vanquished, it is impossible I should, scarce any other spoil I have done him can amount to the value of mine, supposing it equally cultivated and of an extent anyway coming near what I had over-run of his.[3] The destruction of a year's product or two (for it seldom reaches four or five) is the utmost spoil that usually can be done. For as to money and such riches, and treasure taken away, these are none of nature's goods, they have but a fantastical imaginary value: nature has put no such upon them. They are of no more account by her standard, than the wampompeke of the Americans to an European

---

3. Altered in 2nd edition. 1st edition reads: ". . . supposing it of an extent . . . of his and equally cultivated too."

prince, or the silver money of Europe would have been formerly to an American. And five years' product is not worth the perpetual inheritance of land, where all is possessed, and none remains waste, to be taken up by him that is disseized; which will be easily granted, if one do but take away the imaginary value of money, the disproportion being more than between five and five hundred, though, at the same time, half a year's product is more worth than the inheritance, where, there being more land than the inhabitants possess and make use of, any one has liberty to make use of the waste. But there, conquerors take little care to possess themselves of the lands of the vanquished. No damage, therefore, that men in the state of nature (as all princes and governments are in reference to one another) suffer from one another can give a conqueror power to dispossess the posterity of the vanquished, and turn them out of that inheritance, which ought to be the possession of them and their descendants to all generations. The conqueror, indeed, will be apt to think himself master; and 'tis the very condition of the subdued not to be able to dispute their right. But if that be all, it gives no other title than what bare force gives to the stronger over the weaker, and, by this reason, he that is strongest will have a right to whatever he pleases to seize on.

185. Over those then that joined with him in the war, and over those of the subdued country that opposed him not, and the posterity even of those that did, the conqueror, even in a just war, hath by his conquest no right of dominion; they are free from any subjection to him, and, if their former government be dissolved, they are at liberty to begin and erect another to themselves.

186. The conqueror, 'tis true, usually, by the force he has over them, compels them, with a sword at their breasts, to stoop to his conditions, and submit to such a government as he pleases to afford them; but the enquiry is: What right he has to do so? If it be said they submit by their own consent, then this allows their own consent to be necessary to give the conqueror a title to rule over them. It remains only to be considered whether promises extorted by force, without right, can be thought consent, and how far they bind. To which I shall say, they bind not at all; because, whatsoever another gets from me by force, I still retain the right of, and he is obliged presently to restore. He that forces my horse from me, ought presently to restore him, and I have still a right to retake him. By the same reason, he that forced a promise from me ought presently to restore it, *i.e.*, quit me of the obligation of it; or I may resume it myself, *i.e.*, choose whether I will perform it. For the law of nature, laying an obligation on me only by the rules she prescribes, cannot oblige me by the violation of her rules, such as the extorting anything from me by force. Nor does it at all alter the case to say, I gave

my promise, no more than it excuses the force, and passes the right, when I put my hand in my pocket, and deliver my purse myself to a thief, who demands it with a pistol at my breast.

187. From all which it follows that the government of a conqueror, imposed by force on the subdued, against whom he had no right of war, or who joined not in the war against him, where he had right, has no obligation upon them.

188. But let us suppose that all the men of that community, being all members of the same body politic, may be taken to have joined in that unjust war wherein they are subdued, and so their lives are at the mercy of the conqueror.

189. I say this concerns not their children who are in their minority; for, since a father hath not in himself a power over the life and liberty of his child, no act of his can possibly forfeit it. So that the children, whatever may have happened to the fathers, are freemen, and the absolute power of the conqueror reaches no farther than the persons of the men that were subdued by him, and dies with them; and should he govern them as slaves, subjected to his absolute arbitrary power, he has no such right of dominion over their children. He can have no power over them but by their own consent, whatever he may drive them to say or do; and he has no lawful authority, whilst force, and not choice, compels them to submission.

190. Every man is born with a double right: first, a right of freedom to his person, which no other man has a power over, but the free disposal of it lies in himself; secondly, a right, before any other man, to inherit with his brethren his father's goods.

191. By the first of these a man is naturally free from subjection to any government, though he be born in a place under its jurisdiction; but if he disclaim the lawful government of the country he was born in, he must also quit the right that belonged to him by the laws of it, and the possessions there descending to him from his ancestors, if it were a government made by their consent.

192. By the second, the inhabitants of any country who are descended and derive a title to their estates from those who are subdued, and had a government forced upon them against their free consents, retain a right to the possession of their ancestors, though they consent not freely to the government, whose hard conditions were by force imposed on the possessors of that country. For the first conqueror never having had a title to the land of that country, the people who are the descendants of, or claim under those who were forced to submit to the yoke of a government by constraint, have always a right to shake it off, and free themselves from the usurpation or tyranny which the sword hath brought in upon them, till their rulers put them under such a frame of

government as they willingly and of choice consent to. Who doubts but the Grecian Christians, descendants of the ancient possessors of that country, may justly cast off the Turkish yoke, which they have so long groaned under, whenever they have an opportunity to do it? For no government can have a right to obedience from a people who have not freely consented to it[4]; which they can never be supposed to do till either they are put in a full state of liberty to choose their government and governors, or at least till they have such standing laws, to which they have by themselves or their representatives given their free consent, and also till they are allowed their due property, which is so to be proprietors of what they have, that nobody can take away any part of it without their own consent, without which men, under any government, are not in the state of freemen, but are direct slaves under the force of war.

193. But, granting that the conqueror in a just war has a right to the estates as well as power over the persons of the conquered—which 'tis plain he hath not—nothing of absolute power will follow from hence in the continuance of the government, because the descendants of these being all freemen, if he grants them estates and possessions to inhabit his country (without which it would be worth nothing), whatsoever he grants them, they have, so far as it is granted, property in: the nature whereof is that without a man's own consent it cannot be taken from him.

194. Their persons are free by a native right, and their properties, be they more or less, are their own, and at their own dispose, and not at his; or else it is no property. Supposing the conqueror gives to one man a thousand acres to him and his heirs for ever, to another he lets a thousand acres for his life, under the rent of £50 or £500 per annum, has not the one of these a right to his thousand acres for ever, and the other during his life, paying the said rent? And has not the tenant for life a property in all that he gets over and above his rent, by his labour and industry, during the said term, supposing it be double the rent? Can any one say the king, or conqueror, after his grant, may by his power of conqueror take away all, or part of the land from the heirs of one, or from the other during his life, he paying the rent? Or can he take away from either the goods or money they have got upon the said land, at his pleasure? If he can, then all free and voluntary contracts cease, and are void in the world. There needs nothing to dissolve them at any time but

---

4. Altered in collected edition. Earlier editions read: ". . . of choice consent to, which they can never be supposed . . . ," and place the sentence "And who doubts but the Grecian Christians . . . they have a power to do it?" at the end of the paragraph.

power enough.[5] And all the grants and promises of men in power are but mockery and collusion; for can there be anything more ridiculous than to say, "I give you and yours this for ever"—and that in the surest and most solemn way of conveyance can be devised—and yet it is to be understood that I have a right, if I please, to take it away from you again to-morrow?

195. I will not dispute now whether princes are exempt from the laws of their country, but this I am sure, they owe subjection to the laws of God and nature. No body, no power, can exempt them from the obligations of that eternal law. Those are so great and so strong in the case of promises that omnipotency itself can be tied by them. Grants, promises, and oaths are bonds that hold the Almighty. Whatever some flatterers say to princes of the world, who altogether, with all their people joined to them, are, in comparison of the great God, but as a drop of the bucket, or a dust on the balance—inconsiderable, nothing!

196. The short of the case in conquest is this: the conqueror, if he have a just cause, has a despotical right over the persons of all that actually aided and concurred in the war against him, and a right to make up his damage and cost out of their labour and estates, so he injure not the right of any other. Over the rest of the people, if there were any that consented not to the war, and over the children of the captives themselves, or the possessions of either, he has no power; and so can have by virtue of conquest no lawful title himself to dominion over them, or derive it to his posterity; but is an aggressor, if he attempts upon their properties, and thereby[6] puts himself in a state of war against them, and has no better a right of principality, he, nor any of his successors, than Hingar or Hubba the Danes had here in England, or Spartacus had he conquered Italy would have had[7]; which is to have their yoke cast off as soon as God shall give those under their subjection courage and opportunity to do it. Thus, notwithstanding whatever title the kings of Assyria had over Judah by the sword, God assisted Hezekiah to throw off the dominion of that conquering empire. "And the Lord was with Hezekiah, and he prospered; wherefore he went forth, and he rebelled against the King of Assyria, and served him not" (2 Kings xviii. 7). Whence it is plain that shaking off a power, which force and not right hath set over any one, though it hath the name of rebellion, yet is no offence before God, but is that which he allows and countenances though even promises and covenants, when obtained by force, have in-

---

5. Altered in 2nd edition. 1st edition reads: ". . . nothing but power enough to dissolve . . ."

6. Altered in collected edition. Earlier editions read: ". . . an aggressor, and puts himself . . ."

7. "Would have had" added in collected edition.

tervened. For it is very probable to any one that reads the story of Ahaz and Hezekiah attentively, that the Assyrians subdued Ahaz and deposed him, and made Hezekiah king in his father's lifetime; and that Hezekiah by agreement had done him homage, and paid him tribute all this time.

Chapter XVII

Of Usurpation

197. As conquest may be called a foreign usurpation, so usurpation is a kind of domestic conquest, with this difference, that a usurper can never have right on his side, it being no usurpation but where one is got into the possession of what another has a right to. This, so far as it is usurpation, is a change only of persons, but not of the forms and rules of the government; for if the usurper extend his power beyond what of right belonged to the lawful princes or governors of the commonwealth, 'tis tyranny added to usurpation.

198. In all lawful governments the designation of the persons who are to bear rule is as natural and necessary a part as the form of the government itself, and is that which had its establishment originally from the people; the anarchy being much alike, to have no form of government at all, or to agree that it should be monarchical, but to appoint no way to design the person that shall have the power, and be the monarch[1]. Hence all commonwealths with the form of government established have rules also of appointing those who are to have any share in the public authority, and settled methods of conveying the right to them. For the anarchy is much alike, to have no form of government at all, or to agree that it shall be monarchical but to appoint no way to know or design the person that shall have the power and be the monarch. Whoever gets[1] into the exercise of any part of the power, by other ways than what the laws of the community have prescribed, hath no right to be obeyed, though the form of the commonwealth be still preserved; since he is not the person the laws have appointed, and consequently not the person the people have consented to. Nor can such a usurper, or any deriving from him, ever have a title, till the people are both at liberty to consent, and have actually consented to allow and confirm in him the power he hath till then usurped.

---

1. Altered in collected edition. Earlier editions read: ". . . be the monarch. All commonwealths therefore with the form of government established have rules also of appointing and conveying the right to those who are to have any share in the public authority. And whoever gets . . ."

Chapter XVIII

Of Tyranny

199. As usurpation is the exercise of power which another hath a right to, so tyranny is the exercise of power beyond right, which nobody can have a right to. And this is making use of the power any one has in his hands, not for the good of those who are under it, but for his own private separate advantage. When the governor, however entitled, makes not the law but his will the rule, and his commands and actions are not directed to the preservation of the properties of his people, but the satisfaction of his own ambition, revenge, covetousness, or any other irregular passion.

200. If one can doubt this to be truth or reason, because it comes from the obscure hand of a subject, I hope the authority of a king will make it pass with him. King James the First[1] in his speech to the parliament, 1603, tells them thus: "I will ever prefer the weal of the public and of the whole commonwealth, in making of good laws and constitutions, to any particular and private ends of mine; thinking ever the wealth and weal of the commonwealth to be my greatest weal and worldly felicity; a point wherein a lawful king doth directly differ from a tyrant. For I do acknowledge that the special and greatest point of difference, that is between a rightful king and a usurping tyrant, is this: that whereas the proud and ambitious tyrant doth think his kingdom and people are only ordained for satisfaction of his desires and unreasonable appetites; the righteous and just king doth by the contrary acknowledge himself to be ordained for the procuring of the wealth and property of his people." And again, in his speech to the parliament, 1609, he hath these words: "The king binds himself by a double oath, to the observation of the fundamental laws of his kingdom; tacitly, as by being a king, and so bound to protect as well the people, as the laws of his kingdom, and expressly by his oath at his coronation; so as every just king, in a settled kingdom, is bound to observe that paction made to his people by his laws, in framing his government agreeable thereunto, according to that paction which God made with Noah after the deluge. Hereafter, seedtime and harvest, and cold and heat, and summer and winter, and day and night, shall not cease while the earth remaineth. And therefore a king governing in a settled kingdom leaves to be a king and degenerates into a tyrant, as soon as he leaves off to rule according to his laws." And a little after, "Therefore all kings that are not tyrants, or perjured, will be glad to bound themselves within

---

1. "The First" added in *errata* list in 3rd edition.

the limits of their laws. And they that persuade them the contrary are vipers and pests, both against them and the commonwealth." Thus that learned king, who well understood the notions of things, makes the difference betwixt a king and a tyrant to consist only in this, that one makes the laws the bounds of his power, and the good of the public the end of his government; the other makes all give way to his own will and appetite.

201. 'Tis a mistake to think this fault is proper only to monarchies; other forms of government are liable to it as well as that. For wherever the power, that is put in any hands for the government of the people and the preservation of their properties, is applied to other ends, and made use of to impoverish, harass, or subdue them to the arbitrary and irregular commands of those that have it, there it presently becomes tyranny, whether those that thus use it are one or many. Thus we read of the thirty tyrants at Athens, as well as one at Syracuse; and the intolerable dominion of the Decemviri at Rome was nothing better.

202. Wherever law ends tyranny begins, if the law be transgressed to another's harm. And whosoever in authority exceeds the power given him by the law, and makes use of the force he has under his command to compass that upon the subject which the law allows not, ceases in that to be a magistrate; and, acting without authority, may be opposed as any other man who by force invades the right of another. This is acknowledged in subordinate magistrates. He that hath authority to seize my person in the street, may be opposed as a thief and a robber if he endeavours to break into my house to execute a writ, notwithstanding that I know he has such a warrant and such a legal authority as will empower him to arrest me abroad. And why this should not hold in the highest, as well as in the most inferior magistrate, I would gladly be informed. Is it reasonable that the eldest brother, because he has the greatest part of his father's estate, should thereby have a right to take away any of his younger brothers' portions? Or that a rich man, who possessed a whole country, should from thence have a right to seize, when he pleased, the cottage and garden of his poor neighbour? The being rightfully possessed of great power and riches, exceedingly beyond the greatest part of the sons of Adam, is so far from being an excuse, much less a reason, for rapine and oppression, which the endamaging another without authority is, that it is a great aggravation of it. For the exceeding the bounds of authority is no more a right in a great than in a petty officer, no more justifiable in a king than a constable; but is so much the worse in him, in that he has more trust put in him, has already a much greater share than the rest of his brethren, and is supposed, from the advantages of his education, employment,

and counsellors, to be more knowing in the measures of right and wrong.[2]

203. May the commands then of a prince be opposed? May he be resisted as often as any one shall find himself aggrieved, and but imagine he has not right done him? This will unhinge and overturn all polities, and, instead of government and order, leave nothing but anarchy and confusion.

204. To this I answer, that force is to be opposed to nothing but to unjust and unlawful force; whoever makes any opposition in any other case draws on himself a just condemnation both from God and man, and so no such danger or confusion will follow, as is often suggested. For,

205. First, As, in some countries, the person of the prince by the law is sacred, and so, whatever he commands or does, his person is still free from all question or violence, not liable to force, or any judicial censure or condemnation. But yet opposition may be made to the illegal acts of any inferior officer, or other commissioned by him, unless he will, by actually putting himself into a state of war with his people, dissolve the government, and leave them to that defence which belongs to every one in the state of nature. For of such things who can tell what the end will be? And a neighbour kingdom has shewn the world an odd example. In all other cases the sacredness of the person exempts him from all inconveniencies, whereby he is secure, whilst the government stands, from all violence and harm whatsoever; than which there cannot be a wiser constitution. For the harm he can do in his own person not being likely to happen often, nor to extend itself far; nor being able by his single strength to subvert the laws, nor oppress the body of the people, should any prince have so much weakness and ill nature as to be willing to do it, the inconveniency of some particular mischiefs that may happen sometimes, when a heady prince comes to the throne, are well recompensed by the peace of the public and security of the government in the person of the chief magistrate thus set out of the reach of danger; it being safer for the body that some few private men should be sometimes in danger to suffer than that the head of the republic should be easily and upon slight occasions exposed.

206. Secondly, But this privilege, belonging only to the king's person, hinders not but they may be questioned, opposed, and resisted who use unjust force, though they pretend a commission from him which the law authorizes not. As is plain in the case of him that has the

2. Altered in collected edition. Earlier editions read: ". . . constable; but so much the worse in him as that he has more trust put in him, is supposed, from the advantage of education and counsellors, to have better knowledge and less reason to do it, having already a greater share than the rest of his brethren."

king's writ to arrest a man, which is a full commission from the king; and yet he that has it cannot break open a man's house to do it, nor execute this command of the king upon certain days, nor in certain places, though this commission have no such exception in it; but they are the limitations of the law, which if any one transgress, the king's commission excuses him not. For the king's authority being given him only by the law, he cannot empower any one to act against the law, or justify him by his commission in so doing. The commission or command of any magistrate where he has no authority being as void and insignificant as that of any private man; the difference between the one and the other being that the magistrate has some authority so far and to such ends, and the private man has none at all. For 'tis not the commission, but the authority, that gives the right of acting, and against the laws there can be no authority. But, notwithstanding such resistance, the king's person and authority are still both secured, and so no danger to governor or government.

207. Thirdly, Supposing a government wherein the person of the chief magistrate is not thus sacred, yet this doctrine of the lawfulness of resisting all unlawful exercises of his power will not upon every slight occasion endanger him or embroil the government. For where the injured party may be relieved, and his damages repaired by appeal to the law, there can be no pretence for force, which is only to be used where a man is intercepted from appealing to the law. For nothing is to be accounted hostile force, but where it leaves not the remedy of such an appeal. And 'tis such force alone that puts him that uses it into a state of war, and makes it lawful to resist him. A man with a sword in his hand demands my purse in the highway, when perhaps I have not 12d. in my pocket; this man I may lawfully kill. To another I deliver £100 to hold only whilst I alight, which he refuses to restore me when I am got up again, but draws his sword to defend the possession of it by force if I endeavour[3] to retake it. The mischief this man does me is a hundred, or possibly a thousand times more than the other perhaps intended me (whom I killed before he really did me any), and yet I might lawfully kill the one, and cannot so much as hurt the other lawfully. The reason whereof is plain, because the one using force, which threatened my life, I could not have time to appeal to the law to secure it, and when 'twas gone it was too late to appeal. The law could not restore life to my dead carcase. The loss was irreparable, which to prevent the law of nature gave me a right to destroy him who had put himself into a state of war with me, and threatened my destruction. But in the other case, my

---

3. "If" added in *errata* list in 2nd edition. 1st edition reads: ". . . by force: I endeavour . . ."

life not being in danger, I may have the benefit of appealing to the law, and have reparation for my £100 that way.

208. Fourthly, But if the unlawful acts done by the magistrate be maintained (by the power he has got), and the remedy which is due by law be by the same power obstructed, yet the right of resisting, even in such manifest acts of tyranny, will not suddenly or on slight occasions disturb the government. For if it reach no farther than some private men's cases, though they have a right to defend themselves and recover by force what by unlawful force is taken from them; yet the right to do so will not easily engage them in a contest wherein they are sure to perish; it being as impossible for one or a few oppressed men to disturb the government, where the body of the people do not think themselves concerned in it, as for a raving madman or heady malcontent to overturn a well-settled state, the people being as little apt to follow the one as the other.

209. But if either these illegal acts have extended to the majority of the people; or if the mischief and oppression has lighted only on some few, but in such cases as the precedent and consequences seem to threaten all, and they are persuaded in their consciences, that their laws, and with them their estates, liberties, and lives are in danger, and perhaps their religion too; how they will be hindered from resisting illegal force used against them I cannot tell. This is an inconvenience, I confess, that attends all governments whatsoever, when the governors have brought it to this pass, to be generally suspected of their people; the most dangerous state they can possibly put themselves in, wherein they are the less to be pitied, because it is so easy to be avoided; it being as impossible for a governor, if he really means the good of his people, and the preservation of them and their laws together, not to make them see and feel it, as it is for the father of a family not to let his children see he loves and takes care of them.

210. But if all the world shall observe pretences of one kind and actions of another; arts used to elude the law, and the trust of prerogative (which is an arbitrary power in some things left in the prince's hand to do good, not harm to the people) employed contrary to the end for which it was given: if the people shall find the ministers and subordinate magistrates chosen suitable to such ends, and favoured or laid by proportionably as they promote or oppose them: if they see several experiments made of arbitrary power, and that religion underhand favoured (though publicly proclaimed again) which is readiest to introduce it, and the operators in it supported as much as may be; and when that cannot be done, yet approved still, and liked the better: if a long train of actions[4] shew the councils all tending that way; how can

---

4. Actions: 6th edition. Earlier editions read: "actings."

a man any more hinder himself from being persuaded in his own mind which way things are going, or from casting about how to save himself, than he could from believing the captain of the ship he was in was carrying him and the rest of the company to Algiers, when he found him always steering that course, though cross winds, leaks in his ship, and want of men and provisions did often force him to turn his course another way for some time, which he steadily returned to again as soon as the wind, weather, and other circumstances would let him?

Chapter XIX

Of the Dissolution of Government

211. He that will with any clearness speak of the dissolution of government ought, in the first place, to distinguish between the dissolution of the society and the dissolution of the government. That which makes the community, and brings men out of the loose state of nature into one politic society, is the agreement which every one has with the rest to incorporate and act as one body, and so be one distinct commonwealth. The usual, and almost only way whereby this union is dissolved, is the inroad of foreign force making a conquest upon them. For in that case (not being able to maintain and support themselves as one entire and independent body) the union belonging to that body which consisted therein must necessarily cease, and so every one return to the state he was in before, with a liberty to shift for himself and provide for his own safety as he thinks fit in some other society. Whenever the society is dissolved, it is certain the government of that society cannot remain. Thus conquerors' swords often cut up governments by the roots, and mangle societies to pieces, separating the subdued or scattered multitude from the protection of and dependence on that society which ought to have preserved them from violence. The world is too well instructed in, and too forward to allow of, this way of dissolving of governments, to need any more to be said of it; and there wants not much argument to prove that where the society is dissolved, the government cannot remain—that being as impossible as for the frame of a house to subsist when the materials of it are scattered and displaced by a whirlwind, or jumbled into a confused heap by an earthquake.

212. Besides this overturning from without, governments are dissolved from within.

First, When the legislative is altered. Civil society being a state of peace amongst those who are of it, from whom the state of war is excluded by the umpirage which they have provided in their legislative, for the ending all differences that may arise amongst any of them, 'tis in their legislative that the members of a commonwealth are united and combined together in one coherent living body. This is the soul that gives form, life, and unity to the commonwealth. From hence the several members have their mutual influence, sympathy, and connexion. And, therefore, when the legislative is broken or dissolved, dissolution and death follow. For the essence and union of the society consisting in having one will, the legislative, when once established by the majority, has the declaring and, as it were, keeping of that will. The constitution of the legislative is the first and fundamental act of the society, whereby provision is made for the continuation of their union, under the direction of persons and bonds of laws made by persons authorized thereunto by the consent and appointment of the people, without which no one man or number of men amongst them can have authority of making laws that shall be binding to the rest. When any one or more shall take upon them to make laws, whom the people have not appointed so to do, they make laws without authority, which the people are not therefore bound to obey; by which means they come again to be out of subjection, and may constitute to themselves a new legislative, as they think best, being in full liberty to resist the force of those who without authority would impose anything upon them. Every one is at the disposure of his own will, when those, who had by the delegation of the society the declaring of the public will, are excluded from it, and others usurp the place who have no such authority or delegation.

213. This being usually brought about by such in the commonwealth who misuse the power they have, it is hard to consider it aright, and know at whose door to lay it, without knowing the form of government in which it happens. Let us suppose, then, the legislative placed in the concurrence of three distinct persons.

1. A single hereditary person having the constant supreme executive power, and with it the power of convoking and dissolving the other two within certain periods of time.

2. An assembly of hereditary nobility.

3. An assembly of representatives chosen *pro tempore* by the people. Such a form of government supposed, it is evident,

214. First, That when such a single person or prince sets up his own arbitrary will in place of the laws which are the will of the society, declared by the legislative, then the legislative is changed. For that being in effect the legislative, whose rules and laws are put in execution and required to be obeyed; when other laws are set up, and other rules pretended and enforced, than what the legislative constituted by the society have enacted, 'tis plain that the legislative is changed. Whoever

introduces new laws, not being thereunto authorized by the fundamental appointment of the society, or subverts the old, disowns and overturns the power by which they were made, and so sets up a new legislative.

215. Secondly, When the prince hinders the legislative from assembling in its due time, or from acting freely, pursuant to those ends for which it was constituted, the legislative is altered. For 'tis not a certain number of men, no, nor their meeting, unless they have also freedom of debating and leisure of perfecting what is for the good of the society, wherein the legislative consists. When these are taken away or altered so as to deprive the society of the due exercise of their power, the legislative is truly altered. For it is not names that constitute governments, but the use and exercise of those powers that were intended to accompany them; so that he who takes away the freedom, or hinders the acting of the legislative in its due seasons, in effect takes away the legislative, and puts an end to the government.

216. Thirdly, When, by the arbitrary power of the prince, the electors or ways of elections are altered, without the consent and contrary to the common interest of the people, there also the legislative is altered. For if others than those whom the society hath authorized thereunto do choose, or in another way than what the society hath prescribed, those chosen are not the legislative appointed by the people.

217. Fourthly, The delivery also of the people into the subjection of a foreign power, either by the prince, or by the legislative, is certainly a change of the legislative, and so a dissolution of the government. For the end why people entered into society being to be preserved one entire, free, independent society, to be governed by its own laws, this is lost whenever they are given up into the power of another.

218. Why in such a constitution as this the dissolution of the government in these cases is to be imputed to the prince, is evident; because he, having the force, treasure, and offices of the state to employ, and often persuading himself, or being flattered by others, that as supreme magistrate he is incapable of control, he alone is in a condition to make great advances towards such changes, under pretence of lawful authority, and has it in his hands to terrify or suppress opposers, as factious, seditious, and enemies to the government. Whereas no other part of the legislative or people is capable by themselves to attempt any alteration of the legislative, without open and visible rebellion, apt enough to be taken notice of, which, when it prevails, produces effects very little different from foreign conquest. Besides, the prince in such a form of government, having the power of dissolving the other parts of the legislative, and thereby rendering them private persons, they can never, in opposition to him, or without his concurrence, alter the legislative by a law, his consent being necessary to give

any of their decrees that sanction. But yet so far as the other parts of the legislative any way contribute to any attempt upon the government, and do either promote, or not, what lies in them, hinder such designs, they are guilty, and partake in this, which is certainly the greatest crime men can be guilty of one towards another.

219. There is one way more whereby such a government may be dissolved, and that is, when he who has the supreme executive power neglects and abandons that charge, so that the laws already made can no longer be put in execution. This is demonstratively to reduce all to anarchy, and so effectually to dissolve the government. For laws not being made for themselves, but to be by their execution the bonds of the society, to keep every part of the body politic in its due place and function; when that totally ceases, the government visibly ceases, and the people become a confused multitude without order or connexion. Where there is no longer the administration of justice, for the securing of men's rights, nor any remaining power within the community to direct the force, or provide for the necessities of the public, there certainly is no government left. Where the laws cannot be executed, it is all one as if there were no laws; and a government without laws is, I suppose, a mystery in politics, inconceivable to human capacity, and inconsistent with human society.

220. In these and the like cases, when the government is dissolved, the people are at liberty to provide for themselves by erecting a new legislative, differing from the other, by the change of persons, or form, or both, as they shall find it most for their safety and good. For the society can never, by the fault of another, lose the native and original right it has to preserve itself, which can only be done by a settled legislative, and a fair and impartial execution of the laws made by it. But the state of mankind is not so miserable that they are not capable of using this remedy, till it be too late to look for any. To tell people they may provide for themselves by erecting a new legislative, when by oppression, artifice, or being delivered over to a foreign power, their old one is gone, is only to tell them they may expect relief when it is too late, and the evil is past cure. This is in effect no more than to bid them first be slaves, and then to take care of their liberty; and when their chains are on tell them they may act like freemen. This, if barely so, is rather mockery than relief; and men can never be secure from tyranny if there be no means to escape it till they are perfectly under it. And therefore it is that they have not only a right to get out of it, but to prevent it.

221. There is therefore, secondly, another way whereby governments are dissolved, and that is when the legislative or the prince, either of them, act contrary to their trust.

First, The legislative acts against the trust reposed in them when they endeavour to invade the property of the subject, and to make themselves or any part of the community masters or arbitrary disposers of the lives, liberties, or fortunes of the people.

222. The reason why men enter into society is the preservation of their property; and the end why they choose and authorize a legislative is that there may be laws made, and rules set, as guards and fences to the properties of all the members of the society, to limit the power and moderate the dominion of every part and member of the society. For since it can never be supposed to be the will of the society that the legislative should have a power to destroy that which every one designs to secure by entering into society, and for which the people submitted themselves to legislators of their own making; whenever the legislators endeavour to take away and destroy the property of the people, or to reduce them to slavery under arbitrary power, they put themselves into a state of war with the people, who are thereupon absolved from any farther obedience, and are left to the common refuge which God hath provided for all men against force and violence. Whensoever, therefore, the legislative shall transgress this fundamental rule of society, and either by ambition, fear, folly, or corruption, endeavour to grasp themselves or put into the hands of any other an absolute power over the lives, liberties, and estates of the people, by this breach of trust they forfeit the power the people had put into their hands for quite contrary ends, and it devolves to the people; who have a right to resume their original liberty, and by the establishment of the new legislative (such as they shall think fit) provide for their own safety and security, which is the end for which they are in society. What I have said here concerning the legislative in general, holds true also concerning the supreme executor, who having a double trust put in him, both to have a part in the legislative and the supreme execution of the law, acts against both when he goes about to set up his own arbitrary will as the law of the society. He acts also contrary to his trust when he either employs the force, treasure, and offices of the society, to corrupt the representatives, and gain them to his purposes; or openly pre-engages the electors, and prescribes to their choice such whom he has by solicitations, threats, promises, or otherwise, won to his designs, and employs them to bring in such, who have promised beforehand what to vote and what to enact. Thus to regulate candidates and electors, and new-model the ways of election, what is it but to cut up the government by the roots, and poison the very fountain of public security? For the people having reserved to themselves the choice of their representatives as the fence to their properties, could do it for no other end but that they might always be freely chosen, and, so chosen, freely act and advise as the necessity of the commonwealth and the public good should upon exam-

ination and mature debate be judged to require. This, those who give their votes before they hear the debate, and have weighed the reasons on all sides, are not capable of doing. To prepare such an assembly as this, and endeavour to set up the declared abettors of his own will for the true representatives of the people and the law-makers of the society, is certainly as great a breach of trust, and as perfect a declaration of a design to subvert the government, as is possible to be met with. To which if one shall add rewards and punishments visibly employed to the same end, and all the arts of perverted law made use of to take off and destroy all that stand in the way of such a design, and will not comply and consent to betray the liberties of their country, 'twill be past doubt what is doing. What power they ought to have in the society, who thus employ it contrary to the trust that went along with it in its first institution, is easy to determine; and one cannot but see that he who has once attempted any such thing as this cannot any longer be trusted.

223. To this perhaps it will be said, that the people being ignorant and always discontented, to lay the foundation of government in the unsteady opinion and uncertain humour of the people is to expose it to certain ruin; and no government will be able long to subsist if the people may set up a new legislative whenever they take offence at the old one. To this I answer: Quite the contrary. People are not so easily got out of their old forms as some are apt to suggest. They are hardly to be prevailed with to amend the acknowledged faults in the frame they have been accustomed to. And if there be any original defects, or adventitious ones introduced by time or corruption, 'tis not an easy thing to get them changed, even when all the world sees there is an opportunity for it. This slowness and aversion in the people to quit their old constitutions has, in the many revolutions which have been seen in this kingdom, in this and former ages, still kept us to, or after some interval of fruitless attempts still brought us back again to, our old legislative of King, Lords, and Commons. And whatever provocations have made the crown be taken from some of our princes' heads, they never carried the people so far as to place it in another line.

224. But 'twill be said, this hypothesis lays a ferment for frequent rebellion. To which I answer:

First, No more than any other hypothesis. For when the people are made miserable, and find themselves exposed to the ill-usage of arbitrary power, cry up their governors as much as you will for sons of Jupiter, let them be sacred and divine, descended, or authorized from heaven, give them out for whom or what you please, the same will happen. The people generally ill-treated, and contrary to right, will be ready upon any occasion to ease themselves of a burden that sits heavy upon them. They will wish and seek for the opportunity, which in the change, weakness, and accidents of human affairs, seldom delays long to offer itself. He must have lived but a little while in the world who has not seen examples of this in his time, and he must have read very little who cannot produce examples of it in all sorts of governments in the world.

225. Secondly, I answer, such revolutions happen not upon every little mismanagement in public affairs. Great mistakes in the ruling part, many wrong and inconvenient laws, and all the slips of human frailty, will be borne by the people without mutiny or murmur. But if a long train of abuses, prevarications, and artifices, all tending the same way, make the design visible to the people—and they cannot but feel what they lie under, and see whither they are going—'tis not to be wondered that they should then rouse themselves and endeavour to put the rule into such hands which may secure to them the ends for which government was at first erected; and without which ancient names and specious forms are so far from being better that they are much worse than the state of nature or pure anarchy; the inconveniencies being all as great and as near, but the remedy farther off and more difficult.

226. Thirdly, I answer, that this doctrine of a[1] power in the people of providing for their safety anew by a new legislative, when their legislators have acted contrary to their trust by invading their property, is the best fence against rebellion, and the probablest means to hinder it. For rebellion being an opposition, not to persons, but authority, which is founded only in the constitutions and laws of the government; those, whoever they be, who by force break through, and by force justify their violation of them, are truly and properly rebels. For when men, by entering into society and civil government, have excluded force, and introduced laws for the preservation of property, peace, and unity amongst themselves, those who set up force again in opposition to the laws do *rebellare*—that is, bring back again the state of war—and are properly rebels; which they who are in power (by the pretence they have to authority, the temptation of force they have in their hands, and the flattery of those about them) being likeliest to do, the properest way to prevent the evil is to shew them the danger and injustice of it, who are under the greatest temptation to run into it.

227. In both the fore-mentioned cases, when either the legislative is changed or the legislators act contrary to the end for which they were constituted, those who are guilty are guilty of rebellion. For if any one by force takes away the established legislative of any society, and the laws by them made pursuant to their trust, he thereby takes away the umpirage which every one had consented to for a peaceable decision

---

1. "Doctrine of a" added in collected editions.

of all their controversies, and a bar to the state of war amongst them. They who remove, or change the legislative, take away this decisive power, which nobody can have but by the appointment and consent of the people; and so destroying the authority which the people did, and nobody else can set up, and introducing a power which the people hath not authorized, they actually introduce a state of war, which is that of force without authority. And thus by removing the legislative established by the society (in whose decisions the people acquiesced and united, as to that of their own will), they untie the knot and expose the people anew to the state of war. And if those who by force take away the legislative are rebels, the legislators themselves, as has been shewn, can be no less esteemed so, when they who were set up for the protection and preservation of the people, their liberties and properties, shall by force invade and endeavour to take them away; and so they, putting themselves into a state of war with those who made them the protectors and guardians of their peace, are properly and with the greatest aggravation *rebellantes*, rebels.

228. But if they who say it lays a foundation for rebellion mean that it may occasion civil wars or intestine broils, to tell the people they are absolved from obedience when illegal attempts are made upon their liberties or properties, and may oppose the unlawful violence of those who were their magistrates, when they invade their properties contrary to the trust put in them; and that therefore this doctrine is not to be allowed, being so destructive to the peace of the world: they may as well say upon the same ground that honest men may not oppose robbers or pirates because this may occasion disorder or bloodshed. If any mischief come in such cases, it is not to be charged upon him who defends his own right, but on him that invades his neighbour's. If the innocent honest man must quietly quit all he has, for peace sake, to him who will lay violent hands upon it, I desire it may be considered what a kind of peace there will be in the world, which consists only in violence and rapine, and which is to be maintained only for the benefit of robbers and oppressors. Who would not think it an admirable peace betwixt the mighty and the mean, when the lamb without resistance yielded his throat to be torn by the imperious wolf? Polyphemus's den gives us a perfect pattern of such a peace and such a government, wherein Ulysses and his companions had nothing to do but quietly to suffer themselves to be devoured. And no doubt Ulysses, who was a prudent man, preached up passive obedience, and exhorted them to a quiet submission by representing to them of what concernment peace was to mankind, and by shewing the inconveniencies might happen if they should offer to resist Polyphemus, who had now the power over them.

229. The end of government is the good of mankind; and which is

best for mankind, that the people should be always exposed to the boundless will of tyranny, or that the rulers should be sometimes liable to be opposed when they grow exorbitant in the use of their power, and employ it for the destruction and not the preservation of the properties of their people?

230. Nor let any one say that mischief can arise from hence, as often as it shall please a busy head or turbulent spirit to desire the alteration of the government. 'Tis true such men may stir whenever they please, but it will be only to their own just ruin and perdition. For till the mischief be grown general, and the ill-designs of the rulers become visible, or their attempts sensible to the greater part, the people who are more disposed to suffer than right themselves by resistance are not apt to stir. The examples of particular injustice, or oppression of here and there an unfortunate man, move them not. But if they universally have a persuasion grounded upon manifest evidence that designs are carrying on against their liberties, and the general course and tendency of things cannot but give them strong suspicions of the evil intention of their governors, who is to be blamed for it? Who can help it if they who might avoid it bring themselves into this suspicion? Are the people to be blamed, if they have the sense of rational creatures, and can think of things no otherwise than as they find and feel them? And is it not rather their fault, who put things into such a posture, that they would not have them thought to be as they are? I grant that the pride, ambition, and turbulency of private men have sometimes caused great disorders in commonwealths, and factions have been fatal to states and kingdoms. But whether the mischief hath oftener begun in the people's wantonness, and a desire to cast off the lawful authority of their rulers, or in the rulers' insolence, and endeavours to get and exercise an arbitrary power over their people; whether oppression or disobedience gave the first rise to the disorder, I leave it to impartial history to determine. This I am sure, whoever, either ruler or subject, by force goes about to invade the rights of either prince or people, and lays the foundation for overturning the constitution and frame of any just government, is highly[2] guilty of the greatest crime I think a man is capable of, being to answer for all those mischiefs of blood, rapine, and desolation, which the breaking to pieces of governments brings on a country. And he who does it is justly to be esteemed the common enemy and pest of mankind, and is to be treated accordingly.

231. That subjects or foreigners, attempting by force on the properties of any people, may be resisted with force, is agreed on all hands.

---

2. "Highly" added in collected edition. Earlier editions read: ". . . government, he is guilty of the . . ."

But that magistrates, doing the same thing, may be resisted, hath of late been denied. As if those who had the greatest privileges and advantages by the law, had thereby power to break those laws by which alone they were set in a better place than their brethren. Whereas their offence is thereby the greater, both as being ungrateful for the greater share they have by the law, and breaking also that trust which is put into their hands by their brethren.

232. Whosoever uses force without right, as every one does in society who does it without law, puts himself into a state of war with those against whom he so uses it; and in that state all former ties are cancelled, all other rights cease, and every one has a right to defend himself and to resist the aggressor. This is so evident that Barclay himself, that great assertor of the power and sacredness of kings, is forced to confess, that it is lawful for the people in some cases to resist their king; and that too in a chapter wherein he pretends to shew that the divine law shuts up the people from all manner of rebellion. Whereby it is evident, even by his own doctrine, that, since they may in some cases resist, all resisting of princes is not rebellion. His words are these:—

Quod si quis dicat, Ergone populus tyrannicæ crudelitati et furori jugulum semper præbebit? Ergone multitudo civitates suas fame, ferro, et flammâ vastari, seque, conjuges, et liberos fortunæ ludibrio et tyranni libidini exponi, inque omnia vitæ pericula omnesque miserias et molestias à rege deduci patientur? Num illis, quod omni animantium generi est à naturâ tributum, denegari debet, ut scilicet vim vi repellant, seseque ab injuriâ tueantur? Huic breviter responsum sit, populo universo non negari defensionem, quæ juris naturalis est, neque ultionem quæ præter naturam est adversus regem concedi debere. Quapropter si rex non in singulares tantum personas aliquot privatum odium exerceat, sed corpus etiam reipublicæ, cujus ipse caput est, *i.e.* totum populum, vel insignem aliquam ejus partem, immani et intolerandâ sævitiâ seu tyrannide divexet; populo, quidem hoc casu resistendi ac tuendi se ab injuriâ potestas competit, sed tuendi se tantum, non enim in principem invadendi: et restituendæ injuriæ illatæ, non recedendi à debitâ reverentiâ propter acceptam injuriam. Præsentem denique impetum propulsandi non vim præteritam ulciscendi jus habet. Horum enim alterum à naturâ est, ut vitam scilicet corpusque tueamur. Alterum vero contra naturam, ut inferior de superiori supplicium sumat. Quod itaque populas malum, antequam factum sit, impedire potest, ne fiat, id postquam factum est, in regem authorem sceleris vindicare non potest: populus igitur hoc ampliùs quam privatus quispiam habet: quod huic, vel ipsis adversariis judicibus, excepto Buchanano, nullum nisi in patientia remedium superest. Cum ille si

intolerabilis tyrannis est (modicum enim ferre omnino debet) resistere
cum reverentiâ possit. — Barclay, *Contra Monarchomachos*, lib. iii, c. 8.

In English thus:—

233. But if any one should ask: Must the people, then, always lay
themselves open to the cruelty and rage of tyranny? Must they see their
cities pillaged and laid in ashes, their wives and children exposed to the
tyrant's lust and fury, and themselves and families reduced by their king
to ruin, and all the miseries of want and oppression, and yet sit still?
Must men alone be debarred the common privilege of opposing force
with force, which nature allows so freely to all other creatures for their
preservation from injury? I answer: Self-defence is a part of the law of
nature; nor can it be denied the community, even against the king himself. But to revenge themselves upon him must by no means be allowed
them, it being not agreeable to that law. Wherefore, if the king shall
shew an hatred, not only to some particular persons, but sets himself
against the body of the commonwealth, whereof he is the head, and
shall, with intolerable ill-usage, cruelly tyrannize over the whole or a
considerable part of the people, in this case the people have a right to
resist and defend themselves from injury. But it must be with this caution, that they only defend themselves, but do not attack their prince.
They may repair the damages received, but must not, for any provocation, exceed the bounds of due reverence and respect. They may re-
pulse the present attempt, but must not revenge past violences. For it is
natural for us to defend life and limb; but that an inferior should punish a superior, is against nature. The mischief which is designed them,
the people may prevent before it be done; but when it is done, they
must not revenge it on the king, though author of the villainy. This,
therefore, is the privilege of the people in general, above what any private person hath: that particular men are allowed by our adversaries
themselves (Buchanan only excepted), to have no other remedy but patience; but the body of the people may, with respect, resist intolerable
tyranny; for when it is but moderate, they ought to endure it.

234. Thus far that great advocate of monarchical power allows of resistance.

235. 'Tis true he has annexed two limitations to it to no purpose.

First, He says, it must be with reverence.

Secondly, It must be without retribution or punishment; and the reason he gives is, because an inferior cannot punish a superior.

First, How to resist force without striking again, or how to strike with
reverence, will need some skill to make intelligible. He that shall op-

pose an assault only with a shield to receive the blows, or in any more respectful posture, without a sword in his hand, to abate the confidence and force of the assailant, will quickly be at an end of his resistance, and will find such a defence serve only to draw on himself the worse usage. This is as ridiculous a way of resisting as Juvenal thought it of fighting: *ubi tu pulsas, ego vapulo tantum*. And the success of the combat will be unavoidably the same he there describes it:—

> Libertas pauperis hæc est:
> Pulsatus rogat, et pugnis concisus adorat,
> Ut liceat paucis cum dentibus inde reverti.

This will always be the event of such an imaginary resistance, where men may not strike again. He, therefore, who may resist, must be allowed to strike. And then let our author or anybody else join a knock on the head, or a cut on the face, with as much reverence and respect as he thinks fit. He that can reconcile blows and reverence may, for aught I know, deserve for his pains a civil, respectful cudgelling, wherever he can meet with it.

Secondly, As to his second, An inferior cannot punish a superior; that is true, generally speaking, whilst he is his superior. But to resist force with force, being the state of war that levels the parties, cancels all former relation of reverence, respect, and superiority; and then the odds that remains is, that he who opposes the unjust aggressor has this superiority over him—that he has a right, when he prevails, to punish the offender, both for the breach of the peace, and all the evils that followed upon it. Barclay, therefore, in another place, more coherently to himself, denies it to be lawful to resist a king in any case. But he there assigns two cases whereby a king may un-king himself. His words are:—

Quid ergo, nulline casus incidere possunt quibus populo sese erigere atque in regem impotentius dominantem arma capere et invadere jure suo suâque authoritate liceat? Nulli certe quamdiu rex manet. Semper enim ex divinis id obstat, Regem honorificato; et qui potestati resistit, Dei ordinationi resistit: non aliàs igitur in eum populo potestas est quam si id committat propter quod ipso jure rex esse desinat. Tunc enim se ipse principatu exuit atque in privatis constituit liber; hoc modo populus et superior efficitur, reverso ad eum scilicet jure illo quod ante regem inauguratum in interregno habuit. At sunt paucorum generum commissa ejusmodi quæ hunc effectum pariunt. At ego cum plurima animo perlustrem, duo tantum invenio, duos, inquam, casus quibus rex ipso facto ex rege non regem se facit et omni honore et dignitate regali atque in subditos potestate destituit; quorum etiam meminit Winzerus. Horum unus est, si regnum disperdat, quemadmodum

de Nerone fertur, quod is nempe senatum populumque Romanum
atque adeo urbem ipsam ferro flammaque vastare, ac novas sibi sedes
quærere decrevisset. Et de Caligula, quod palam denunciarit se neque
civem neque principem senatui amplius fore, inque animo habuerit,
interempto utriusque ordinis electissimo, quoque Alexandriam commi-
grare, ac ut populum uno ictu interimeret, unam ei cervicem optavit.
Talia cum rex aliquis meditatur et molitur serio, omnem regnandi
curam et animum ilico abjicit, ac proinde imperium in subditos amit-
tit, ut dominus servi pro derelicto habiti dominium.

236. Alter casus est, si rex in alicujus clientelam se contulit, ac regnum quod liberum à majoribus et populo traditum accepit, alienæ di-
tioni mancipavit. Nam tunc quamvis forte non eâ mente id agit populo
plane ut incommodet; tamen quia quod præcipuum est regiæ dignitatis
amisit, ut summus scilicet in regno secundum Deum sit, et solo Deo
inferior, atque populum etiam totum ignorantem vel invitum, cujus
libertatem sartam et tectam conservare debuit, in alterius gentis di-
tionem et potestatem dedidit; hâc velut quadam regni abalienatione ef-
fecit, ut nec quod ipse in regno imperium habuit retineat, nec in eum
cui collatum voluit, juris quicquam transferat; atque ita eo facto
liberum jam et suæ potestatis populum relinquit, cujus rei exemplum
unum annales Scotici uppeditant. — Barclay, *Contra Monarchomachos*,
l. iii, c. 16.

Which in English runs thus[3]: —

237. What, then, can there no case happen wherein the people may
of right and by their own authority help themselves take arms, and set
upon their king imperiously domineering over them? None at all whilst
he remains a king: "Honour the king," and "He that resists the power
resists the ordinance of God," are divine oracles that will never permit
it. The people, therefore, can never come by a power over him, unless
he does something that makes him cease to be a king; for then he divests himself of his crown and dignity, and returns to the state of a private man, and the people become free and superior, the power which
they had in the interregnum, before they crowned him king, devolving
to them again. But there are but few miscarriages which bring the matter to this state. After considering it well on all sides, I can find but two.
Two cases there are, I say, whereby a king *ipso facto* becomes no king,
and loses all power and regal authority over his people, which are also
taken notice of by Winzerus.

The first is, if he endeavour to overturn the government—that is, if

---

3. Altered in 2nd edition. 1st edition reads: "Which may be thus Englished."

he have a purpose and design to ruin the kingdom and common-wealth, as it is recorded of Nero that he resolved to cut off the senate and people of Rome, lay the city waste with fire and sword, and then remove to some other place. And of Caligula, that he openly declared that he would be no longer a head to the people or senate, and that he had it in his thoughts to cut off the worthiest men of both ranks, and then retire to Alexandria; and he wished that the people had but one neck that he might despatch them all at a blow. Such designs as these, when any king harbours in his thoughts and seriously promotes, he im-mediately gives up all care and thought of the commonwealth, and consequently forfeits the power of governing his subjects, as a master does the dominion over his slaves whom he hath abandoned.

238. The other case is, when a king makes himself dependent of an-other, and subjects his kingdom, which his ancestors left him, and the people put free into his hands, to the dominion of another; for, how-ever perhaps it may not be his intention to prejudice the people, yet be-cause he has hereby lost the principal part of regal dignity, viz., to be, next and immediately under God, supreme in his kingdom, and also because he betrayed or forced his people, whose liberty he ought to have carefully preserved, into the power and dominion of a foreign na-tion. By this, as it were, alienation of his kingdom, he himself loses the power he had in it before, without transferring any the least right to those on whom he would have bestowed it; and so by this act sets the people free, and leaves them at their own disposal. One example of this is to be found in the Scotch annals.

239. In these cases Barclay, the great champion of absolute monar-chy, is forced to allow that a king may be resisted and ceases to be a king. That is, in short, not to multiply cases, in whatsoever he has no authority, there he is no king and may be resisted; for wheresoever the authority ceases, the king ceases too, and becomes like other men who have no authority. And these two cases he instances in, differ little from those above-mentioned, to be destructive to governments, only that he has omitted the principle from which his doctrine flows; and that is the breach of trust in not preserving the form of government agreed on, and in not intending the end of government itself, which is the public good and preservation of property. When a king has dethroned himself and put himself in a state of war with his people, what shall hinder them from prosecuting him who is no king, as they would any other man who has put himself into a state of war with them? Barclay, and those of his opinion, would do well to tell us. This[4] farther I desire may

---

4. See note 5.

be taken notice of out of Barclay, that he says, the mischief that is de-signed them, the people may prevent before it be done: whereby he al-lows resistance when tyranny is but in design. Such designs as these (says he) when any king harbours in his thoughts and seriously pro-motes, he immediately gives up all care and thought of the common-wealth; so that, according to him, the neglect of the public good is to be taken as an evidence of such design, or at least for a sufficient cause of resistance. And the reason of all he gives in these words, Because he betrayed or forced his people whose liberty he ought carefully to have preserved. What he adds, into the power and dominion of a foreign na-tion, signifies nothing, the fault and forfeiture lying in the loss of their liberty which he ought to have preserved, and not in any distinction of the persons to whose dominion they were subjected. The people's right is equally invaded and their liberty lost whether they are made slaves to any of their own or a foreign nation; and in this lies the injury, and against this only have they the right of defence. And there are instances to be found in all countries which shew that 'tis not the change of na-tions in the persons of their governors, but the change of government that gives the offence.[5] Bilson, a bishop of our church, and a great stick-ler for the power and prerogative of princes, does, if I mistake not, in his treatise of *Christian Subjection*, acknowledge that princes may for-feit their power and their title to the obedience of their subjects; and if there needed authority in a case where reason is so plain, I could send my reader to Bracton, Fortescue, and the author of *The Mirror*, and oth-ers, writers that cannot be suspected to be ignorant of our government or enemies to it. But I thought Hooker alone might be enough to sat-isfy those men who, relying on him for their ecclesiastical polity, are by a strange fate carried to deny those principles upon which he builds it. Whether they are herein made the tools of cunninger workmen, to pull down their own fabric, they were best look. This I am sure, their civil policy is so new, so dangerous, and so destructive to both rulers and people that, as former ages never could bear the broaching of it, so, it may be hoped, those to come, redeemed from the impositions of those Egyptian under-taskmasters, will abhor the memory of such servile flat-terers, who, whilst it seemed to serve their turn, resolved all govern-ment into absolute tyranny, and would have all men born to what their mean souls fitted them for, slavery.

240. Here, 'tis like, the common question will be made: Who shall be judge whether the prince or legislative act contrary to their trust? This, perhaps, ill-affected and factious men may spread amongst the people, when the prince only makes use of his due prerogative. To this

---

5. The words "This farther I desire . . . gives the offence" were added in the 2nd edition.

I reply: The people shall be judge; for who shall be judge whether his trustee or deputy acts well, and according to the trust reposed in him, but he who deputes him, and must, by having deputed him, have still a power to discard him when he fails in his trust? If this be reasonable in particular cases of private men, why should it be otherwise in that of the greatest moment, where the welfare of millions is concerned, and also where the evil, if not prevented, is greater, and the redress very difficult, dear, and dangerous?

241. But farther, this question, who shall be judge, cannot mean that there is no judge at all; for where there is no judicature on earth to decide controversies amongst men, God in heaven is judge. He alone, 'tis true, is judge of the right; but every man is judge for himself, as in all other cases, so in this, whether another hath put himself into a state of war with him, and whether he should appeal to the Supreme Judge, as Jephtha did.

242. If a controversy arise betwixt a prince and some of the people, in a matter where the law is silent or doubtful, and the thing be of great consequence, I should think the proper umpire in such a case should be the body of the people; for in cases where the prince hath a trust reposed in him, and is dispensed from the common ordinary rules of the law; there, if any men find themselves aggrieved, and think the prince acts contrary to or beyond that trust, who so proper to judge as the body of the people (who at first lodged that trust in him) how far they meant it should extend? But if the prince, or whoever they be in the administration, decline that way of determination, the appeal then lies nowhere but to heaven; force between either persons who have no known superior on earth, or which permits no appeal to a judge on earth, being properly a state of war, wherein the appeal lies only to heaven; and in that state the injured party must judge for himself when he will think fit to make use of that appeal and put himself upon it.

243. To conclude, the power that every individual gave the society, when he entered into it, can never revert to the individuals again as long as the society lasts, but will always remain in the community; because without this there can be no community, no commonwealth, which is contrary to the original agreement; so also when the society hath placed the legislative in any assembly of men, to continue in them and their successors, with direction and authority for providing such successors, the legislative can never revert to the people whilst that government lasts; because having provided a legislative with power to continue for ever, they have given up their political power to the legislative and cannot resume it. But if they have set limits to the duration of their legislative, and made this supreme power in any person or assembly only temporary; or else, when by the miscarriages of those in authority

it is forfeited; upon the forfeiture, or at the determination of the time set, it reverts to the society, and the people have a right to act as supreme, and continue the legislative in themselves; or erect a new form, or under the old form place it in new hands[6], as they think good.

---

6. Altered in collected edition. Earlier editions read: "or place it in a new form, or new hands . . ."

A Letter Concerning Toleration

Ea est summa ratio et sapientia boni civis, commoda civium non divellere atque omnes aequitate eâdem continere.—Cicero, *de Officiis*.

To the Reader

The ensuing letter concerning toleration, first printed in Latin this very year in Holland, has already been translated both into Dutch and French. So general and speedy an approbation may, therefore, bespeak its favourable reception in England. I think, indeed, there is no nation under heaven in which so much has already been said upon that subject as ours. But yet, certainly, there is no people that stand in more need of having something further both said and done amongst them in this point than we do.

Our government has not only been partial in matters of religion; but those also who have suffered under that partiality, and have therefore endeavoured by their writings to vindicate their own rights and liberties, have for the most part done it upon narrow principles, suited only to the interests of their own sects.

This narrowness of spirit, on all sides, has undoubtedly been the principal occasion of our miseries and confusions. But, whatever have been the occasion, it is now high time to seek for a thorough cure. We have need of more generous remedies than what have yet been made use of, in our distemper. It is neither declarations of indulgence, nor acts of comprehension, such as have yet been practised or projected amongst us, that can do the work. The first will but palliate, the second increase our evil.

Absolute liberty, just and true liberty, equal and impartial liberty, is the thing that we stand in need of. Nor, though this has indeed been much talked of, I doubt it has not been much understood; I am sure not at all practised, either by our governors towards the people in general, or by any dissenting parties of the people towards one another.

I cannot, therefore, but hope that this discourse, which treats of that subject, however briefly, yet more exactly than any we have yet seen, demonstrating both the equitableness and practicableness of the thing, will be esteemed highly seasonable by all men that have souls large enough to prefer the true interest of the public before that of a party.

It is for the use of such as are already so spirited, or to inspire that spirit into those that are not, that I have translated it into our language. But the thing itself is so short that it will not bear a longer preface. I leave it, therefore, to the consideration of my countrymen, and heartily wish they may make the use of it that it appears to be designed for.

[This Preface is probably the work of William Popple, the translator.]

114

A Letter Concerning Toleration

Honoured Sir,

Since you are pleased to inquire what are my thoughts about the mutual toleration of Christians in their different professions of religion, I must needs answer you freely, that I esteem that toleration to be the chief characteristic mark of the true church. For whatsoever some people boast of the antiquity of places and names, or of the pomp of their outward worship; others, of the reformation of their discipline; all, of the orthodoxy of their faith—for every one is orthodox to himself—these things, and all others of this nature, are much rather marks of men striving for power and empire over one another, than of the church of Christ. Let any one have never so true a claim to all these things, yet if he be destitute of charity, meekness, and good-will in general towards all mankind, even to those that are not Christians, he is certainly yet short of being a true Christian himself. "The kings of the Gentiles exercise lordship over them," said our Saviour to his disciples, "but ye shall not be so" (Luke xxii. 25). The business of true religion is quite another thing. It is not instituted in order to the erecting of an external pomp, nor to the obtaining of ecclesiastical dominion, nor to the exercising of compulsive force, but to the regulating of men's lives, according to the rules of virtue and piety. Whosoever will list himself under the banner of Christ, must in the first place, and above all things, make war upon his own lusts and vices. It is in vain for any man to usurp the name of Christian, without holiness of life, purity of manners, benignity and meekness of spirit. "Let every one that nameth the name of Christ, depart from iniquity" (2 Tim. ii. 19). "Thou, when thou art converted, strengthen thy brethren," said our Lord to Peter (Luke xxii. 32). It would, indeed, be very hard for one that appears careless about his own salvation to persuade me that he were extremely concerned for mine. For it is impossible that those should sincerely and heartily apply themselves to make other people Christians, who have not really embraced the Christian religion in their own hearts. If the Gospel and the apostles may be credited, no man can be a Christian without charity, and without that faith which works, not by force, but by love. Now, I appeal to the consciences of those that persecute, torment, destroy, and kill other men upon pretence of religion, whether they do it out of friendship and kindness towards them or no? And I shall then indeed, and not until then, believe they do so, when I shall see those fiery zealots correcting, in the same manner, their friends and familiar acquaintance for the manifest sins they commit against the precepts of the Gospel; when I shall see them persecute with fire and sword the members of their own communion that are tainted with enormous vices, and without amendment are in danger of eternal perdition; and when I shall see them thus express their love and desire of the salvation of their souls by the infliction of torments, and exercise of all manner of cruelties. For if it be out of a principle of charity, as they pretend, and love to men's souls, that they deprive them of their estates, maim them with corporal punishments, starve and torment them in noisome prisons, and in the end even take away their lives,— I say, if all this be done merely to make men Christians, and procure their salvation, why then do they suffer whoredom, fraud, malice, and such-like enormities, which (according to the apostle (Rom. i)) manifestly relish of heathenish corruption, to predominate so much and abound amongst their flocks and people? These, and such-like things, are certainly more contrary to the glory of God, to the purity of the church, and to the salvation of souls, than any conscientious dissent from ecclesiastical decisions, or separation from public worship, whilst accompanied with innocence of life. Why then does this burning zeal for God, for the church, and for the salvation of souls—burning, I say, literally, with fire and faggot—pass by those moral vices and wickednesses without any chastisement, which are acknowledged by all men to be diametrically opposite to the profession of Christianity, and bend all its nerves either to the introducing of ceremonies, or to the establishment of opinions, which for the most part are about nice and intricate matters, that exceed the capacity of ordinary understandings? Which of the parties contending about these things is in the right, which of them is guilty of schism or heresy, whether those that domineer or those that suffer, will then at last be manifest, when the causes of their separation come to be judged of. He, certainly, that follows Christ, embraces his doctrine, and bears his yoke, though he forsake both father and mother, separate from the public assemblies and ceremonies of his country, or whomsoever or whatsoever else he relinquishes, will not then be judged a heretic.

Now, though the divisions that are amongst sects should be allowed to be never so obstructive of the salvation of souls; yet, nevertheless, adultery, fornication, uncleanliness, lasciviousness, idolatry, and such-like things, cannot be denied to be works of the flesh, concerning which the apostle has expressly declared (Gal. v.) that "they who do them shall not inherit the kingdom of God." Whosoever, therefore, is sincerely solicitous about the kingdom of God, and thinks it his duty to endeavour the enlargement of it amongst men, ought to apply himself with no less care and industry to the rooting out of these immoralities than to the extirpation of sects. But if any one do otherwise, and whilst he is cruel and implacable towards those that differ from him in opinion, he be indulgent to such iniquities and immoralities as are unbecoming the name of a Christian, let such a one talk never so much of the church, he plainly demonstrates by his actions that it is another kingdom he aims at, and not the advancement of the kingdom of God.

That any man should think fit to cause another man—whose salvation he heartily desires—to expire in torments, and that even in an unconverted state, would, I confess, seem very strange to me, and, I think, to any other also. But nobody, surely, will ever believe that such a carriage can proceed from charity, love, or good-will. If any one maintain that men ought to be compelled by fire and sword to profess certain doctrines, and conform to this or that exterior worship, without any regard had unto their morals; if any one endeavour to convert those that are erroneous unto the faith, by forcing them to profess things that they do not believe, and allowing them to practise things that the Gospel does not permit, it cannot be doubted indeed but such a one is desirous to have a numerous assembly joined in the same profession with himself; but that he principally intends by those means to compose a truly Christian church, is altogether incredible. It is not, therefore, to be wondered at if those who do not really contend for the advancement of the true religion, and of the church of Christ, make use of arms that do not belong to the Christian warfare. If, like the Captain of our salvation, they sincerely desired the good of souls, they would tread in the steps and follow the perfect example of that Prince of peace, who sent out his soldiers to the subduing of nations, and gathering them into his church, not armed with the sword, or other instruments of force, but prepared with the Gospel of peace, and with the exemplary holiness of their conversation. This was his method. Though if infidels were to be converted by force, if those that are either blind or obstinate were to be drawn off from their errors by armed soldiers, we know very well that it was much more easy for him to do it with armies of heavenly legions, than for any son of the church, how potent soever, with all his dragoons.

The toleration of those that differ from others in matters of religion, is so agreeable to the Gospel of Jesus Christ, and to the genuine reason of mankind, that it seems monstrous for men to be so blind as not to perceive the necessity and advantage of it in so clear a light. I will not here tax the pride and ambition of some, the passion and uncharitable zeal of others. These are faults from which human affairs can perhaps scarce ever be perfectly freed; but yet such as nobody will bear the plain imputation of, without covering them with some specious colour;

and so pretend to commendation, whilst they are carried away by their own irregular passions. But, however, that some may not colour their spirit of persecution and unchristian cruelty with a pretence of care of the public weal and observation of the laws; and that others, under pretence of religion, may not seek impunity for their libertinism and licentiousness; in a word, that none may impose either upon himself or others, by the pretences of loyalty and obedience to the prince, or of tenderness and sincerity in the worship of God I esteem it above all things necessary to distinguish exactly the business of civil government from that of religion, and to settle the just bound that lie between the one and the other. If this be not done, there can be no end put to the controversies that will be always arising between those that have, or at least pretend to have, on the one side, a concernment for the interest of men's souls, and, on the other side, a care of the commonwealth.

The commonwealth seems to me to be a society of men constituted only for the procuring, preserving, and advancing their own civil interests.

Civil interests I call life, liberty, health, and indolency of body; and the possession of outward things, such as money, lands, houses, furniture, and the like.

It is the duty of the civil magistrate, by the impartial execution of equal laws, to secure unto all the people in general, and to every one of his subjects in particular, the just possession of these things belonging to this life. If any one presume to violate the laws of public justice and equity, established for the preservation of those things, his presumption is to be checked by the fear of punishment, consisting of the deprivation or diminution of those civil interests, or goods, which otherwise he might and ought to enjoy. But seeing no man does willingly suffer himself to be punished by the deprivation of any part of his goods, and much less of his liberty or life, therefore is the magistrate armed with the force and strength of all his subjects, in order to the punishment of those that violate any other man's rights.

Now that the whole jurisdiction of the magistrate reaches only to these civil concernments, and that all civil power, right, and dominion, is bounded and confined to the only care of promoting these things; and that it neither can nor ought in any manner to be extended to the salvation of souls, these following considerations seem unto me abundantly to demonstrate.

First, because the care of souls is not committed to the civil magistrate, any more than to other men. It is not committed unto him, I say, by God; because it appears not that God has ever given any such authority to one man over another, as to compel any one to his religion. Nor can any such power be vested in the magistrate by the consent of the people, because no man can so far abandon the care of his own salvation as blindly to leave to the choice of any other, whether prince or subject, to prescribe to him what faith or worship he shall embrace. For no man can, if he would, conform his faith to the dictates of another. All the life and power of true religion consist in the inward and full persuasion of the mind; and faith is not faith without believing. Whatever profession we make, to whatever outward worship we conform, if we are not fully satisfied in our own mind that the one is true, and the other well pleasing unto God, such profession and such practice, far from being any furtherance, are indeed great obstacles to our salvation. For in this manner, instead of expiating other sins by the exercise of religion, I say, in offering thus unto God Almighty such a worship as we esteem to be displeasing unto him, we add unto the number of our other sins those also of hypocrisy, and contempt of his Divine Majesty.

In the second place, the care of souls cannot belong to the civil magistrate, because his power consists only in outward force; but true and saving religion consists in the inward persuasion of the mind, without which nothing can be acceptable to God. And such is the nature of the understanding, that it cannot be compelled to the belief of anything by outward force. Confiscation of estate, imprisonment, torments, nothing of that nature can have any such efficacy as to make men change the inward judgment that they have framed of things.

It may indeed be alleged that the magistrate may make use of arguments, and thereby draw the heterodox into the way of truth, and procure their salvation. I grant it; but this is common to him with other men. In teaching, instructing, and redressing the erroneous by reason, he may certainly do what becomes any good man to do. Magistracy does not oblige him to put off either humanity or Christianity; but it is one thing to persuade, another to command; one thing to press with arguments, another with penalties. This civil power alone has a right to do; to the other good-will is authority enough. Every man has commission to admonish, exhort, convince another of error, and, by reasoning, to draw him into truth; but to give laws, receive obedience, and compel with the sword, belongs to none but the magistrate. And upon this ground, I affirm that the magistrate's power extends not to the establishing of any articles of faith, or forms of worship, by the force of his laws. For laws are of no force at all without penalties, and penalties in this case are absolutely impertinent, because they are not proper to convince the mind. Neither the profession of any articles of faith, nor the conformity to any outward form of worship (as has been already said), can be available to the salvation of souls, unless the truth of the one, and the acceptableness of the other unto God, be thoroughly believed by those that so profess and practise. But penalties are no way capable to produce such belief. It is only light and evidence that can work a change in men's opinions; which light can in no manner proceed from corporal sufferings, or any other outward penalties.

In the third place, the care of the salvation of men's souls cannot belong to the magistrate; because, though the rigour of laws and the force of penalties were capable to convince and change men's minds, yet would not that help at all to the salvation of their souls. For there being but one truth, one way to heaven, what hope is there that more men would be led into it if they had no rule but the religion of the court, and were put under the necessity to quit the light of their own reason, and oppose the dictates of their own consciences, and blindly to resign themselves up to the will of their governors, and to the religion which either ignorance, ambition, or superstition had chanced to establish in the countries where they were born? In the variety and contradiction of opinions in religion, wherein the princes of the world are as much divided as in their secular interests, the narrow way would be much straitened; one country alone would be in the right, and all the rest of the world put under an obligation of following their princes in the ways that lead to destruction; and that which heightens the absurdity, and very ill suits the notion of a Deity, men would owe their eternal happiness or misery to the places of their nativity.

These considerations, to omit many others that might have been urged to the same purpose, seem unto me sufficient to conclude that all the power of civil government relates only to men's civil interests, is confined to the care of the things of this world, and hath nothing to do with the world to come.

Let us now consider what a church is. A church, then, I take to be a voluntary society of men, joining themselves together of their own accord in order to the public worshipping of God in such manner as they judge acceptable to him, and effectual to the salvation of their souls.

I say it is a free and voluntary society. Nobody is born a member of any church; otherwise the religion of parents would descend unto children by the same right of inheritance as their temporal estates, and every one would hold his faith by the same tenure he does his lands, than which nothing can be imagined more absurd. Thus, therefore, that matter stands. No man by nature is bound unto any particular church or sect, but every one joins himself voluntarily to that society in which he believes he has found that profession and worship which is truly acceptable to God. The hope of salvation, as it was the only cause of his entrance into that communion, so it can be the only reason of his stay there. For if afterwards he discover anything either erroneous in the doctrine or incongruous in the worship of that society to which he has joined himself, why should it not be as free for him to go out as it was to enter? No member of a religious society can be tied with any other bonds but what proceed from the certain expectation of eternal life. A church, then, is a society of members voluntarily uniting to that end.

It follows now that we consider what is the power of this church, and unto what laws it is subject.

Forasmuch as no society, how free soever, or upon whatsoever slight occasion instituted, whether of philosophers for learning, of merchants for commerce, or of men of leisure for mutual conversation and discourse, no church or company, I say, can in the least subsist and hold together, but will presently dissolve and break in pieces, unless it be regulated by some laws, and the members all consent to observe some order. Place and time of meeting must be agreed on; rules for admitting and excluding members must be established; distinction of officers, and putting things into a regular course, and such-like, cannot be omitted. But since the joining together of several members into this church-society, as has already been demonstrated, is absolutely free and spontaneous, it necessarily follows that the right of making its laws can belong to none but the society itself; or, at least (which is the same thing), to those whom the society by common consent has authorized thereunto.

Some, perhaps, may object that no such society can be said to be a true church unless it have in it a bishop or presbyter, with ruling authority derived from the very apostles, and continued down to the present times by an uninterrupted succession.

To these I answer: In the first place, let them show me the edict by which Christ has imposed that law upon his church. And let not any man think me impertinent, if in a thing of this consequence I require that the terms of that edict be very express and positive; for the promise he has made us (Matt. xviii. 20), that wheresoever two or three are gathered together in his name, he will be in the midst of them, seems to imply the contrary. Whether such an assembly want anything necessary to a true church, pray do you consider. Certain I am that nothing can be there wanting unto the salvation of souls, which is sufficient to our purpose.

Next, pray observe how great have always been the divisions amongst even those who lay so much stress upon the divine institution and continued succession of a certain order of rulers in the church. Now, their very dissension unavoidably puts us upon a necessity of deliberating, and, consequently, allows a liberty of choosing that which upon consideration we prefer.

And, in the last place, I consent that these men have a ruler in their church, established by such a long series of succession as they judge necessary, provided I may have liberty at the same time to join myself to that society in which I am persuaded those things are to be found which are necessary to the salvation of my soul. In this manner ecclesiastical liberty will be preserved on all sides, and no man will have a legislator imposed upon him but whom himself has chosen.

But since men are so solicitous about the true church, I would only ask them here, by the way, if it be not more agreeable to the church of Christ to make the conditions of her communion consist in such things, and such things only, as the Holy Spirit has in the Holy Scriptures declared, in express words, to be necessary to salvation; I ask, I say, whether this be not more agreeable to the church of Christ than for men to impose their own inventions and interpretations upon others as if they were of divine authority, and to establish by ecclesiastical laws, as absolutely necessary to the profession of Christianity, such things as the Holy Scriptures do either not mention, or at least not expressly command? Whosoever requires those things in order to ecclesiastical communion, which Christ does not require in order to life eternal, he may, perhaps, indeed constitute a society accommodated to his own opinion and his own advantage; but how that can be called the church of Christ which is established upon laws that are not his, and which excludes such persons from its communion as he will one day receive into the kingdom of heaven, I understand not. But this being not a proper place to inquire into the marks of the true church, I will only mind those that contend so earnestly for the decrees of their own society, and that cry out continually, The church! the church! with as much noise, and perhaps upon the same principle, as the Ephesian silversmiths did for their Diana; this, I say, I desire to mind them of, that the Gospel frequently declares that the true disciples of Christ must suffer persecution; but that the church of Christ should persecute others, and force others by fire and sword to embrace her faith and doctrine, I could never yet find in any of the books of the New Testament.

The end of a religious society (as has already been said) is the public worship of God, and, by means thereof, the acquisition of eternal life. All discipline ought therefore to tend to that end, and all ecclesiastical laws to be thereunto confined. Nothing ought nor can be transacted in this society relating to the possession of civil and worldly goods. No force is here to be made use of upon any occasion whatsoever. For force belongs wholly to the civil magistrate, and the possession of all outward goods is subject to his jurisdiction.

But, it may be asked, by what means then shall ecclesiastical laws be established, if they must be thus destitute of all compulsive power? I answer: They must be established by means suitable to the nature of such things, whereof the external profession and observation—if not

proceeding from a thorough conviction and approbation of the mind—
is altogether useless and unprofitable. The arms by which the members
of this society are to be kept within their duty are exhortations, admonitions, and advices. If by these means the offenders will not be re-
claimed, and the erroneous convinced, there remains nothing further
to be done but that such stubborn and obstinate persons, who give no
ground to hope for their reformation, should be cast out and separated
from the society. This is the last and utmost force of ecclesiastical authority. No other punishment can thereby be inflicted than that, the relation ceasing between the body and the member which is cut off. The
person so condemned ceases to be a part of that church.

These things being thus determined, let us inquire, in the next place:
How far the duty of toleration extends, and what is required from every
one by it?

And, first, I hold that no church is bound, by the duty of toleration,
to retain any such person in her bosom as, after admonition, continues
obstinately to offend against the laws of the society. For these being the
condition of communion and the bond of the society, if the breach of
them were permitted without any animadversion, the society would immediately be thereby dissolved. But, nevertheless, in all such cases care
is to be taken that the sentence of excommunication, and the execution thereof, carry with it no rough usage of word or action whereby the
ejected person may any wise be damnified in body or estate. For all
force (as has often been said) belongs only to the magistrate, nor ought
any private persons at any time to use force, unless it be in self-defence
against unjust violence. Excommunication neither does, nor can, deprive the excommunicated person of any of those civil goods that he
formerly possessed. All those things belong to the civil government, and
are under the magistrate's protection. The whole force of excommunication consists only in this: that the resolution of the society in that respect being declared, the union that was between the body and some
member comes thereby to be dissolved; and that relation ceasing, the
participation of some certain things which the society communicated
to its members, and unto which no man has any civil right, comes also
to cease. For there is no civil injury done unto the excommunicated
person by the church minister's refusing him that bread and wine, in
the celebration of the Lord's Supper, which was not bought with his
but other men's money.

Secondly, no private person has any right in any manner to prejudice
another person in his civil enjoyments because he is of another church
or religion. All the rights and franchises that belong to him as a man,
or as a denizen, are inviolably to be preserved to him. These are not the
business of religion. No violence nor injury is to be offered him,

whether he be Christian or Pagan. Nay, we must not content ourselves with the narrow measures of bare justice; charity, bounty, and liberality must be added to it. This the Gospel enjoins, this reason directs, and this that natural fellowship we are born into requires of us. If any man err from the right way, it is his own misfortune, no injury to thee; nor therefore art thou to punish him in the things of this life because thou supposest he will be miserable in that which is to come.

What I say concerning the mutual toleration of private persons differing from one another in religion, I understand also of particular churches which stand, as it were, in the same relation to each other as private persons among themselves: nor has any one of them any manner of jurisdiction over any other; no, not even when the civil magistrate (as it sometimes happens) comes to be of this or the other communion. For the civil government can give no new right to the church, nor the church to the civil government. So that whether the magistrate join himself to any church, or separate from it, the church remains always as it was before—a free and voluntary society. It neither requires the power of the sword by the magistrate's coming to it, nor does it lose the right of instruction and excommunication by his going from it. This is the fundamental and immutable right of a spontaneous society—that it has power to remove any of its members who transgress the rules of its institution; but it cannot, by the accession of any new members, acquire any right of jurisdiction over those that are not joined with it. And therefore peace, equity, and friendship are always mutually to be observed by particular churches, in the same manner as by private persons, without any pretence of superiority or jurisdiction over one another.

That the thing may be made clearer by an example, let us suppose two churches—the one of Arminians, the other of Calvinists—residing in the city of Constantinople. Will any one say that either of these churches has a right to deprive the members of the other of their estates and liberty (as we see practised elsewhere), because of their differing from it in some doctrines and ceremonies, whilst the Turks in the meanwhile silently stand by, and laugh to see with what inhuman cruelty Christians thus rage against Christians? But if one of these churches hath this power of treating the other ill, I ask which of them it is to whom that power belongs, and by what right? It will be answered, undoubtedly, that it is the orthodox church which has the right of authority over the erroneous or heretical. This is, in great and specious words, to say just nothing at all. For every church is orthodox to itself; to others, erroneous or heretical. For whatsoever any church believes, it believes to be true; and the contrary unto those things, it pronounces to be error. So that the controversy between these churches about the truth of their doctrines, and the purity of their worship, is on both sides equal; nor is there any judge, either at Constantinople or elsewhere upon earth, by whose sentence it can be determined. The decision of that question belongs only to the Supreme Judge of all men, to whom also alone belongs the punishment of the erroneous. In the meanwhile, let those men consider how heinously they sin, who, adding injustice, if not to their error, yet certainly to their pride, do rashly and arrogantly take upon them to misuse the servants of another master, who are not at all accountable to them.

Nay, further: if it could be manifest which of these two dissenting churches were in the right, there would not accrue thereby unto the orthodox any right of destroying the other. For churches have neither any jurisdiction in worldly matters, nor are fire and sword any proper instruments wherewith to convince men's minds of error, and inform them of the truth. Let us suppose, nevertheless, that the civil magistrate inclined to favour one of them, and to put his sword into their hands, that (by his consent) they might chastise the dissenters as they pleased. Will any man say that any right can be derived unto a Christian church over its brethren from a Turkish emperor? An infidel, who has himself no authority to punish Christians for the articles of their faith, cannot confer such an authority upon any society of Christians, nor give unto them a right which he has not himself. This would be the case at Constantinople; and the reason of the thing is the same in any Christian kingdom. The civil power is the same in every place. Nor can that power, in the hands of a Christian prince, confer any greater authority upon the church than in the hands of a heathen; which is to say, just none at all.

Nevertheless, it is worthy to be observed and lamented that the most violent of these defenders of the truth, the opposers of errors, the exclaimers against schism, do hardly ever let loose this their zeal for God, with which they are so warmed and inflamed, unless where they have the civil magistrate on their side. But so soon as ever court favour has given them the better end of the staff, and they begin to feel themselves the stronger, then presently peace and charity are to be laid aside. Otherwise they are religiously to be observed. Where they have not the power to carry on persecution and to become master, there they desire to live upon fair terms, and preach up toleration. When they are not strengthened with the civil power, then they can bear most patiently and unmovedly the contagion of idolatry, superstition, and heresy in their neighbourhood; of which on other occasions the interest of religion makes them to be extremely apprehensive. They do not forwardly attack those errors which are in fashion at court or are countenanced by the government. Here they can be content to spare their arguments;

which yet (with their leave) is the only right method of propagating truth, which has no such way of prevailing as when strong arguments and good reason are joined with the softness of civility and good usage.

Nobody, therefore, in fine, neither single persons nor churches, nay, nor even commonwealths, have any just title to invade the civil rights and worldly goods of each other upon pretence of religion. Those that are of another opinion would do well to consider with themselves how pernicious a seed of discord and war, how powerful a provocation to endless hatreds, rapines, and slaughters they thereby furnish unto mankind. No peace and security, no, not so much as common friendship, can ever be established or preserved amongst men so long as this opinion prevails, that dominion is founded in grace and that religion is to be propagated by force of arms.

In the third place, let us see what the duty of toleration requires from those who are distinguished from the rest of mankind (from the laity, as they please to call us) by some ecclesiastical character and office; whether they be bishops, priests, presbyters, ministers, or however else dignified or distinguished. It is not my business to inquire here into the original of the power or dignity of the clergy. This only I say, that whencesoever their authority be sprung, since it is ecclesiastical, it ought to be confined within the bounds of the church, nor can it in any manner be extended to civil affairs, because the church itself is a thing absolutely separate and distinct from the commonwealth. The boundaries on both sides are fixed and immovable. He jumbles heaven and earth together, the things most remote and opposite, who mixes these two societies, which are in their original, end, business, and in everything perfectly distinct and infinitely different from each other. No man, therefore, with whatsoever ecclesiastical office he be dignified, can deprive another man that is not of his church and faith either of liberty or of any part of his worldly goods upon the account of that difference between them in religion. For whatsoever is not lawful to the whole church cannot by any ecclesiastical right become lawful to any of its members.

But this is not all. It is not enough that ecclesiastical men abstain from violence and rapine and all manner of persecution. He that pretends to be a successor of the apostles, and takes upon him the office of teaching, is obliged also to admonish his hearers of the duties of peace and good-will towards all men, as well towards the erroneous as the orthodox; towards those that differ from them in faith and worship as well as towards those that agree with them therein. And he ought industriously to exhort all men, whether private persons or magistrates (if any such there be in his church), to charity, meekness, and toleration, and diligently endeavour to ally and temper all that heat and unreasonable averseness of mind which either any man's fiery zeal for his own sect or the craft of others has kindled against dissenters. I will not undertake to represent how happy and how great would be the fruit, both in church and state, if the pulpits everywhere sounded with this doctrine of peace and toleration, lest I should seem to reflect too severely upon those men whose dignity I desire not to detract from, nor would have it diminished either by others or themselves. But this I say, that thus it ought to be. And if any one that professes himself to be a minister of the word of God, a preacher of the gospel of peace, teach otherwise, he either understands not or neglects the business of his calling, and shall one day give account thereof unto the Prince of peace. If Christians are to be admonished that they abstain from all manner of revenge, even after repeated provocations and multiplied injuries, how much more ought they who suffer nothing, who have had no harm done them, forbear violence and abstain from all manner of ill-usage towards those from whom they have received none! This caution and temper they ought certainly to use towards those who mind only their own business, and are solicitous for nothing but that (whatever men think of them) they may worship God in that manner which they are persuaded is acceptable to him, and in which they have the strongest hopes of eternal salvation. In private domestic affairs, in the management of estates, in the conservation of bodily health, every man may consider what suits his own convenience, and follow what course he likes best. No man complains of the ill-management of his neighbour's affairs. No man is angry with another for an error committed in sowing his land or in marrying his daughter. Nobody corrects a spendthrift for consuming his substance in taverns. Let any man pull down, or build, or make whatsoever expenses he pleases, nobody murmurs, nobody controls him; he has his liberty. But if any man do not frequent the church, if he do not there conform his behaviour exactly to the accustomed ceremonies, or if he brings not his children to be initiated in the sacred mysteries of this or the other congregation, this immediately causes an uproar. The neighbourhood is filled with noise and clamour. Every one is ready to be the avenger of so great a crime, and the zealots hardly have the patience to refrain from violence and rapine so long till the cause be heard, and the poor man be, according to form, condemned to the loss of liberty, goods, or life. Oh, that our ecclesiastical orators of every sect would apply themselves with all the strength of arguments that they are able to the confounding of men's errors! But let them spare their persons. Let them not supply their want of reasons with the instruments of force, which belong to another jurisdiction, and do ill become a churchman's hands. Let them not call in the magistrate's authority to the aid of their eloquence or learning, lest perhaps, whilst they pretend only love for the truth, this their intemperate zeal, breathing nothing but fire and sword, betray their ambition and show that what they desire is temporal dominion. For it will be very difficult to persuade men of sense that he who with dry eyes and satisfaction of mind can deliver his brother to the executioner to be burnt alive, does sincerely and heartily concern himself to save that brother from the flames of hell in the world to come.

In the last place, let us now consider what is the magistrate's duty in the business of toleration, which certainly is very considerable.

We have already proved that the care of souls does not belong to the magistrate. Not a magisterial care, I mean (if I may so call it), which consists in prescribing by laws and compelling by punishments. But a charitable care, which consists in teaching, admonishing, and persuading, cannot be denied unto any man. The care, therefore, of every man's soul belongs unto himself, and is to be left unto himself. But what if he neglect the care of his soul? I answer: What if he neglect the care of his health or of his estate, which things are nearlier related to the government of the magistrate than the other? Will the magistrate provide by an express law that such a one shall not become poor or sick? Laws provide, as much as is possible, that the goods and health of subjects be not injured by the fraud and violence of others; they do not guard them from the negligence or ill-husbandry of the possessors themselves. No man can be forced to be rich or healthful whether he will or no. Nay, God himself will not save men against their wills. Let us suppose, however, that some prince were desirous to force his subjects to accumulate riches, or to preserve the health and strength of their bodies. Shall it be provided by law that they must consult none but Roman physicians, and shall every one be bound to live according to their prescriptions? What, shall no potion, no broth, be taken, but what is prepared either in the Vatican, suppose, or in a Geneva shop? Or, to make these subjects rich, shall they all be obliged by law to become merchants or musicians? Or, shall every one turn victualler, or smith, because there are some that maintain their families plentifully and grow rich in those professions? But, it may be said, there are a thousand ways to wealth, but only one way to heaven. It is well said, indeed, especially by those that plead for compelling men into this or the other way. For if there were several ways that led thither, there would not be so much as a pretence left for compulsion. But now if I be marching on with my utmost vigour in that way which, according to the sacred geography, leads straight to Jerusalem, why am I beaten and ill-used by others because, perhaps, I wear not buskins; because my hair is not of the right cut; because, perhaps, I have not been dipped in the right fashion; because I eat flesh upon the road, or some other food which agrees with my stomach; because I avoid certain by-ways, which seem unto me to lead into briars or precipices; because, amongst the several paths that are in the same road, I choose that to walk in which seems to be the straightest and cleanest; because I avoid to keep company with some travellers that are less grave, and others that are more sour than they ought to be; or, in fine, because I follow a guide that either is, or is not, clothed in white, or crowned with a mitre? Certainly, if we consider right, we shall find that, for the most part, they are such frivolous things as these that (without any prejudice to religion or the salvation of souls, if not accompanied with superstition or hypocrisy) might either be observed or omitted. I say, they are such-like things as these which breed implacable enmities amongst Christian brethren, who are all agreed in the substantial and truly fundamental part of religion.

But let us grant unto these zealots, who condemn all things that are not of their mode, that from these circumstances are different ends. What shall we conclude from thence? There is only one of these which is the true way to eternal happiness: but in this great variety of ways that men follow, it is still doubted which is the right one. Now, neither the care of the commonwealth, nor the right enacting of laws, does discover this way that leads to heaven more certainly to the magistrate than every private man's search and study discovers it unto himself. I have a weak body, sunk under a languishing disease, for which (I suppose) there is one only remedy, but that unknown. Does it therefore belong unto the magistrate to prescribe me a remedy, because there is but one, and because it is unknown? Because there is but one way for me to escape death, will it therefore be safe for me to do whatsoever the magistrate ordains? Those things that every man ought sincerely to inquire into himself, and by meditation, study, search, and his own endeavours, attain the knowledge of, cannot be looked upon as the peculiar possession of any sort of men. Princes, indeed, are born superior unto other men in power, but in nature equal. Neither the right nor the art of ruling does necessarily carry along with it the certain knowledge of other things, and least of all of true religion. For if it were so, how could it come to pass that the lords of the earth should differ so vastly as they do in religious matters? But let us grant that it is probable the way to eternal life may be better known by a prince than by his subjects, or at least that in this incertitude of things the safest and most commodious way for private persons is to follow his dictates. You will say, what then? If he should bid you follow merchandise for your livelihood, would you decline that course for fear it should not succeed? I answer: I would turn merchant upon the prince's command, because in case I should have ill-success in trade, he is abundantly able to make up my loss some other way. If it be true, as he pretends, that he desires

I should thrive and grow rich, he can set me up again when unsuccessful voyages have broken me. But this is not the case in the things that regard the life to come; if there I take a wrong course, if in that respect I am once undone, it is not in the magistrate's power to repair my loss, to ease my suffering, nor to restore me in any measure, much less entirely to a good estate. What security can be given for the kingdom of heaven?

Perhaps some will say that they do not suppose this infallible judgment, that all men are bound to follow in the affairs of religion, to be in the civil magistrate, but in the church. What the church has determined, that the civil magistrate orders to be observed; and he provides by his authority that nobody shall either act or believe in the business of religion otherwise than the church teaches. So that the judgment of those things is in the church; the magistrate himself yields obedience thereunto, and requires the like obedience from others. I answer: Who sees not how frequently the name of the church, which was venerable in time of the apostles, has been made use of to throw dust in the people's eyes, in the following ages? But, however, in the present case it helps us not. The one only narrow way which leads to heaven is not better known to the magistrate than to private persons, and therefore I cannot safely take him for my guide, who may probably be as ignorant of the way as myself, and who certainly is less concerned for my salvation than I myself am. Amongst so many kings of the Jews, how many of them were there whom any Israelite, thus blindly following, had not fallen into idolatry, and thereby into destruction? Yet nevertheless, you bid me be of good courage, and tell me that all is now safe and secure, because the magistrate does not now enjoin the observance of his own decrees in matters of religion, but only the decrees of the church. Of what church, I beseech you? of that, certainly, which likes him best. As if he that compels me by laws and penalties to enter into this or the other church, did not interpose his own judgment in the matter. What difference is there whether he lead me himself, or deliver me over to be led by others? I depend both ways upon his will, and it is he that determines both ways of my eternal state. Would an Israelite, that had worshipped Baal upon the command of his king, have been in any better condition, because somebody had told him that the king ordered nothing in religion upon his own head, nor commanded anything to be done by his subjects in divine worship but what was approved by the counsel of priests, and declared to be of divine right by the doctors of their church? If the religion of any church become therefore true and saving, because the head of that sect, the prelates and priests, and those of that tribe, do all of them, with all their might, extol and praise it, what religion can ever be accounted erroneous, false, and destructive?

I am doubtful concerning the doctrine of the Socinians, I am suspicious of the way of worship practised by the Papists, or Lutherans; will it be ever a jot safer for me to join either unto the one or the other of those churches, upon the magistrate's command, because he commands nothing in religion but by the authority and counsel of the doctors of that church?

But, to speak the truth, we must acknowledge that the church (if a convention of clergymen, making canons, must be called by that name) is for the most part more apt to be influenced by the court than the court by the church. How the church was under the vicissitude of orthodox and Arian emperors is very well known. Or if those things be too remote, our modern English history affords us fresh examples in the reigns of Henry VIII, Edward VI, Mary, and Elizabeth, how easily and smoothly the clergy changed their decrees, their articles of faith, their form of worship, everything according to the inclination of those kings and queens. Yet were those kings and queens of such different minds in point of religion, and enjoined thereupon such different things, that no man in his wits (I had almost said none but an atheist) will presume to say that any sincere and upright worshipper of God could, with a safe conscience, obey their several decrees. To conclude, it is the same thing whether a king that prescribes laws to another man's religion, pretend to do it by his own judgment, or by the ecclesiastical authority and advice of others. The decision of churchmen, whose differences and disputes are sufficiently known, cannot be any sounder or safer than his; nor can all their suffrages joined together add a new strength to the civil power. Though this also must be taken notice of—that princes seldom have any regard to the suffrages of ecclesiastics that are not favourers of their own faith and way of worship.

But, after all, the principal consideration, and which absolutely determines this controversy, is this: Although the magistrate's opinion in religion be sound, and the way that he appoints be truly evangelical, yet, if I be not thoroughly persuaded thereof in my own mind, there will be no safety for me in following it. No way whatsoever that I shall walk in against the dictates of my conscience will ever bring me to the mansions of the blessed. I may grow rich by an art that I take not delight in, I may be cured of some disease by remedies that I have not faith in; but I cannot be saved by a religion that I distrust, and by a worship that I abhor. It is in vain for an unbeliever to take up the outward show of another man's profession. Faith only, and inward sincerity, are the things that procure acceptance with God. The most likely and most approved remedy can have no effect upon the patient if his stomach reject it as soon as taken; and you will in vain cram a medicine down a sick man's throat, which his particular constitution will be sure to turn into poison. In a word, whatsoever may be doubtful in religion, yet this at least is certain, that no religion which I believe not to be true can be either true or profitable unto me. In vain, therefore, do princes compel their subjects to come into their church communion, under pretence of saving their souls. If they believe, they will come of their own accord; if they believe not, their coming will nothing avail them. How great soever, in fine, may be the pretence of good-will and charity, and concern for the salvation of men's souls, men cannot be forced to be saved whether they will or no. And therefore, when all is done, they must be left to their own consciences.

Having thus at length freed men from all dominion over one another in matters of religion, let us now consider what they are to do. All men know and acknowledge that God ought to be publicly worshipped; why otherwise do they compel one another unto the public assemblies? Men, therefore, constituted in this liberty are to enter into some religious society, that they meet together, not only for mutual edification, but to own to the world that they worship God, and offer unto his Divine Majesty such service as they themselves are not ashamed of, and such as they think not unworthy of him, nor unacceptable to him; and finally, that by the purity of doctrine, holiness of life, and decent form of worship, they may draw others unto the love of the true religion, and perform such other things in religion as cannot be done by each private man apart.

These religious societies I call churches; and these, I say, the magistrate ought to tolerate, for the business of these assemblies of the people is nothing but what is lawful for every man in particular to take care of—I mean the salvation of their souls; nor in this case is there any difference between the national church and other separated congregations.

But as in every church there are two things especially to be considered—the outward form and rites of worship, and the doctrines and articles of faith—these things must be handled each distinctly, that so the whole matter of toleration may the more clearly be understood.

Concerning outward worship, I say, in the first place, that the magistrate has no power to enforce by law, either in his own church, or much less in another, the use of any rites or ceremonies whatsoever in the worship of God. And this, not only because these churches are free societies, but because whatsoever is practised in the worship of God is only so far justifiable as it is believed by those that practise it to be acceptable unto him. Whatsoever is not done with that assurance of faith is neither well in itself, nor can it be acceptable to God. To impose such things, therefore, upon any people, contrary to their own judgment, is in effect to command them to offend God, which, considering that the end of all religion is to please him, and that liberty is essentially necessary to that end, appears to be absurd beyond expression.

But perhaps it may be concluded from hence that I deny unto the magistrate all manner of power about indifferent things, which, if it be not granted, the whole subject-matter of law-making is taken away. No, I readily grant that indifferent things, and perhaps none but such, are subjected to the legislative power. But it does not therefore follow that the magistrate may ordain whatsoever he pleases concerning anything that is indifferent. The public good is the rule and measure of all law-making. If a thing be not useful to the commonwealth, though it be never so indifferent, it may not presently be established by law.

And further, things never so indifferent in their own nature, when they are brought into the church and worship of God, are removed out of the reach of the magistrate's jurisdiction, because in that use they have no connection at all with civil affairs. The only business of the church is the salvation of souls, and it no way concerns the common-wealth, or any member of it, that this or the other ceremony be there made use of. Neither the use nor the omission of any ceremonies in those religious assemblies does either advantage or prejudice the life, liberty, or estate of any man. For example, let it be granted that the washing of an infant with water is in itself an indifferent thing, let it be granted also that the magistrate understand such washing to be profitable to the curing or preventing of any disease the children are subject unto, and esteem the matter weighty enough to be taken care of by a law. In that case he may order it to be done. But will any one therefore say that a magistrate has the same right to ordain by law that all children shall be baptized by priests in the sacred font in order to the purification of their souls? The extreme difference of these two cases is visible to every one at first sight. Or let us apply the last case to the child of a Jew, and the thing speaks itself. For what hinders but a Christian magistrate may have subjects that are Jews? Now, if we acknowledge that such an injury may not be done unto a Jew as to compel him, against his own opinion, to practise in his religion a thing that is in its nature indifferent, how can we maintain that anything of this kind may be done to a Christian?

Again, things in their own nature indifferent cannot, by any human authority, be made any part of the worship of God—for this very reason: because they are indifferent. For, since indifferent things are not capable, by any virtue of their own, to propitiate the Deity, no human power or authority can confer on them so much dignity and excellency as to enable them to do it. In the common affairs of life that use of indifferent things which God has not forbidden is free and lawful, and therefore in those things human authority has place. But it is not so in matters of religion. Things indifferent are not otherwise lawful in the worship of God than as they are instituted by God himself, and as he, by some positive command, has ordained them to be made a part of that worship which he will vouchsafe to accept at the hands of poor sinful men. Nor, when an incensed Deity shall ask us, "Who has required these, or such-like things at your hands?" will it be enough to answer him that the magistrate commanded them. If civil jurisdiction extend thus far, what might not lawfully be introduced into religion? What hodgepodge of ceremonies, what superstitious inventions, built upon the magistrate's authority, might not (against conscience) be imposed upon the worshippers of God? For the greatest part of these ceremonies and superstitions consists in the religious use of such things as are in their own nature indifferent; nor are they sinful upon any other account than because God is not the author of them. The sprinkling of water, and the use of bread and wine, are both in their own nature and in the ordinary occasions of life altogether indifferent. Will any man therefore say that these things could have been introduced into religion, and made a part of divine worship, if not by divine institution? If any human authority or civil power could have done this, why might it not also enjoin the eating of fish and drinking of ale in the holy banquet as a part of divine worship? Why not the sprinkling of the blood of beasts in churches, and expiations by water or fire, and abundance more of this kind? But these things, how indifferent soever they be in common uses, when they come to be annexed unto divine worship, without divine authority, they are as abominable to God as the sacrifice of a dog. And why is a dog so abominable? What difference is there between a dog and a goat, in respect of the divine nature, equally and infinitely distant from all affinity with matter, unless it be that God required the use of one in his worship, and not of the other? We see, therefore, that indifferent things, how much soever they be under the power of the civil magistrate, yet cannot, upon that pretence, be introduced into religion, and imposed upon religious assemblies, because, in the worship of God, they wholly cease to be indifferent. He that worships God does it with design to please him and procure his favour. But that cannot be done by him who, upon the command of another, offers unto God that which he knows will be displeasing to him, because not commanded by himself. This is not to please God, or appease his wrath, but willingly and knowingly to provoke him by a manifest contempt, which is a thing absolutely repugnant to the nature and end of worship.

But it will be here asked: "If nothing belonging to divine worship be left to human discretion, how is it then that churches themselves have the power of ordering anything about the time and place of worship, and the like?" To this I answer, that in religious worship we must distinguish between what is part of the worship itself and what is but a circumstance. That is a part of the worship which is believed to be appointed by God, and to be well-pleasing to him, and therefore that is necessary. Circumstances are such things which, though in general they cannot be separated from worship, yet the particular instances or modifications of them are not determined, and therefore they are indifferent. Of this sort are the time and place of worship, habit, and posture of him that worships. These are circumstances, and perfectly indifferent, where God has not given any express command about them. For example: amongst the Jews the time and place of their worship, and the habits of those that officiated in it, were not mere circumstances, but a part of the worship itself, in which if anything were defective, or different from the institution, they could not hope that it would be accepted by God. But these, to Christians under the liberty of the Gospel, are mere circumstances of worship, which the prudence of every church may bring into such use as shall be judged most subservient to the end of order, decency, and edification. But, even under the Gospel, those who believe the first or the seventh day to be set apart by God, and consecrated still to his worship, to them that portion of time is not a simple circumstance, but a real part of divine worship, which can neither be changed nor neglected.

In the next place: As the magistrate has no power to impose by his laws the use of any rites and ceremonies in any church, so neither has he any power to forbid the use of such rites and ceremonies as are already received, approved, and practised by any church; because, if he did so, he would destroy the church itself: the end of whose institution is only to worship God with freedom after its own manner.

You will say, by this rule, if some congregations should have a mind to sacrifice infants, or (as the primitive Christians were falsely accused) lustfully pollute themselves in promiscuous uncleanness, or practise any other such heinous enormities, is the magistrate obliged to tolerate them, because they are committed in a religious assembly? I answer, No. These things are not lawful in the ordinary course of life, nor in any private house; and therefore neither are they so in the worship of God, or in any religious meeting. But, indeed, if any people congregated upon account of religion should be desirous to sacrifice a calf, I deny that that ought to be prohibited by a law. Melibœus, whose calf it is, may lawfully kill his calf at home, and burn any part of it that he thinks fit. For no injury is thereby done to any one, no prejudice to another man's goods. And for the same reason he may kill his calf also in a religious meeting. Whether the doing so be well-pleasing to God or no, it is their part to consider that do it. The part of the magistrate is only to take care that the commonwealth receive no prejudice, and that there be no injury done to any man, either in life or estate. And thus what may be spent on a feast may be spent on a sacrifice. But if peradventure such were the state of things that the interest of the commonwealth required all slaughter of beasts should be forborne for some while, in order to the increasing of the stock of cattle that had been destroyed by some extraordinary murrain, who sees not that the magistrate, in such a case, may forbid all his subjects to kill any calves for any use whatsoever? Only it is to be observed that, in this case, the law is not made about a religious, but a political matter; nor is the sacrifice, but the slaughter of calves, thereby prohibited.

By this we see what difference there is between the church and the commonwealth. Whatsoever is lawful in the commonwealth cannot be prohibited by the magistrate in the church. Whatsoever is permitted unto any of his subjects for their ordinary use, neither can nor ought to be forbidden by him to any sect of people for their religious uses. If any man may lawfully take bread or wine, either sitting or kneeling in his own house, the law ought not to abridge him of the same liberty in his religious worship; though in the church the use of bread and wine be very different, and be there applied to the mysteries of faith and rites of divine worship. But those things that are prejudicial to the commonweal of a people in their ordinary use, and are therefore forbidden by laws, those things ought not to be permitted to churches in their sacred rites. Only the magistrate ought always to be very careful that he do not misuse his authority to the oppression of any church, under pretence of public good.

It may be said, what if a church be idolatrous, is that also to be tolerated by the magistrate? I answer, what power can be given to the magistrate for the suppression of an idolatrous church, which may not in time and place be made use of to the ruin of an orthodox one? For it must be remembered that the civil power is the same everywhere, and the religion of every prince is orthodox to himself. If, therefore, such a power be granted unto the civil magistrate in spirituals, as that at Geneva, for example, he may extirpate, by violence and blood, the religion which is there reputed idolatrous, by the same rule another magistrate, in some neighbouring country, may oppress the reformed religion, and, in India, the Christian. The civil power can either change everything in religion, according to the prince's pleasure, or it can change nothing. If it be once permitted to introduce anything into religion, by the means of laws and penalties, there can be no bounds put to it; but it will in the same manner be lawful to alter everything, according to that rule of truth which the magistrate has framed unto himself. No man whatsoever ought therefore to be deprived of his terrestrial enjoyments upon account of his religion. Not even Americans, subjected unto a Christian prince, are to be punished either in body or goods for not embracing our faith and worship. If they are persuaded that they please God in observing the rites of their own country, and that they shall obtain happiness by that means, they are to be left unto God and themselves. Let us trace this matter to the bottom. Thus it is: an inconsiderable and weak number of Christians, destitute of everything, arrive in a Pagan country; these foreigners beseech the inhabitants, by the bowels of humanity, that they would succour them with the necessaries of life; those necessaries are given them, habitations are granted, and they all join together, and grow up into one body of people. The Christian religion by this means takes root in that country, and spreads itself, but does not suddenly grow the strongest. While things are in this condition peace, friendship, faith, and equal justice are preserved amongst them. At length the magistrate becomes a Christian, and by that means their party becomes the most powerful. Then immediately all compacts are to be broken, all civil rights to be violated, that idolatry may be extirpated; and unless these innocent Pagans, strict observers of the rules of equity and the law of nature, and no ways offending against the laws of the society, I say, unless they will forsake their ancient religion, and embrace a new and strange one, they are to be turned out of the lands and possessions of their forefathers, and perhaps deprived of life itself. Then, at last, it appears what zeal for the church, joined with the desire of dominion, is capable to produce, and how easily the pretence of religion, and of the care of souls, serves for a cloak to covetousness, rapine, and ambition.

Now whosoever maintains that idolatry is to be rooted out of any place by laws, punishments, fire, and sword, may apply this story to himself. For the reason of the thing is equal, both in America and Europe. And neither Pagans there, nor any dissenting Christians here, can, with any right, be deprived of their worldly goods by the predominating faction of a court-church; nor are any civil rights to be either changed or violated upon account of religion in one place more than another.

But idolatry, say some, is a sin, and therefore not to be tolerated. If they said it were therefore to be avoided, the inference were good. But it does not follow, that because it is a sin it ought therefore to be punished by the magistrate. For it does not belong unto the magistrate to make use of his sword in punishing everything, indifferently, that he takes to be a sin against God. Covetousness, uncharitableness, idleness, and many other things are sins, by the consent of men, which yet no man ever said were to be punished by the magistrate. The reason is, because they are not prejudicial to other men's rights, nor do they break the public peace of societies. Nay, even the sins of lying and perjury are nowhere punishable by laws; unless, in certain cases, in which the real turpitude of the thing and the offence against God are not considered, but only the injury done unto men's neighbours and to the commonwealth. And what if in another country, to a Mahometan or a Pagan prince, the Christian religion seem false and offensive to God; may not the Christians for the same reason, and after the same manner, be extirpated there?

But it may be urged farther, that, by the law of Moses, idolaters were to be rooted out. True, indeed, by the law of Moses; but that is not obligatory to us Christians. Nobody pretends that everything generally enjoined by the law of Moses ought to be practised by Christians, but there is nothing more frivolous than that common distinction of moral, judicial, and ceremonial law, which men ordinarily make use of. For no positive law whatsoever can oblige any people but those to whom it is given. "Hear, O Israel," sufficiently restrains the obligations of the law of Moses only to that people. And this consideration alone is answer enough unto those that urge the authority of the law of Moses for the inflicting of capital punishment upon idolaters. But, however, I will examine this argument a little more particularly.

The case of idolaters, in respect of the Jewish commonwealth, falls under a double consideration. The first is of those who, being initiated in the Mosaical rites, and made citizens of that commonwealth, did afterwards apostatize from the worship of the God of Israel. These were proceeded against as traitors and rebels, guilty of no less than high treason. For the commonwealth of the Jews, different in that from all others, was an absolute theocracy; nor was there, or could there be, any difference between that commonwealth and the church. The laws established there concerning the worship of one invisible Deity were the civil laws of that people, and a part of their political government, in which God himself was the legislator. Now, if any one can show me where there is a commonwealth at this time, constituted upon that foundation, I will acknowledge that the ecclesiastical laws do there unavoidably become a part of the civil, and that the subjects of that government both may, and ought to be kept in strict conformity with that church by the civil power. But there is absolutely no such thing under the Gospel as a Christian commonwealth. There are, indeed, many cities and kingdoms that have embraced the faith of Christ, but they have retained their ancient form of government, with which the law of Christ hath not at all meddled. He, indeed, hath taught men how, by faith and good works, they may obtain eternal life; but he instituted no commonwealth. He prescribed unto his followers no new and peculiar form of government, not put he the sword into any magistrate's hand, with commission to make use of it in forcing men to forsake their former religion and receive his.

Secondly, foreigners, and such as were strangers to the commonwealth of Israel, were not compelled by force to observe the rites of the Mosaical law; but, on the contrary, in the very same place where it is ordered that an Israelite that was an idolater should be put to death (Exod. xxii. 20, 21), there it is provided that strangers should not be vexed nor oppressed. I confess that the seven nations that possessed the land which was promised to the Israelites were utterly to be cut off; but this was not singly because they were idolaters. For if that had been the reason, why were the Moabites and other nations to be spared? No: the reason is this. God being in a peculiar manner the King of the Jews, he could not suffer the adoration of any other deity (which was properly an act of high treason against himself) in the land of Canaan, which was his kingdom. For such a manifest revolt could no ways consist with his dominion, which was perfectly political in that country. All idolatry was therefore to be rooted out of the bounds of his kingdom, because it was an acknowledgment of another god, that is to say, another king, against the laws of empire. The inhabitants were also to be driven out, that the entire possession of the land might be given to the Israelites. And for the like reason the Emims and the Horims were driven out of their countries by the children of Esau and Lot; and their lands, upon the same grounds, given by God to the invaders (Deut. ii). But, though all idolatry was thus rooted out of the land of Canaan, yet every idolater was not brought to execution. The whole family of Rahab, the whole nation of the Gibeonites, articled with Joshua, and were allowed by treaty; and there were many captives amongst the Jews who were idolaters. David and Solomon subdued many countries without the confines of the land of promise, and carried their conquests as far as Euphrates. Amongst so many captives taken, so many nations reduced under their obedience, we find not one man forced into the Jewish religion and the worship of the true God, and punished for idolatry, though all of them were certainly guilty of it. If any one indeed, becoming a proselyte, desired to be made a denizen of their commonwealth, he was obliged to submit to their laws; that is, to embrace their religion. But this he did willingly, on his own accord, not by constraint. He did not unwillingly submit, to show his obedience, but he sought and solicited for it as a privilege. And, as soon as he was admitted, he became subject to the laws of the commonwealth, by which all idolatry was forbidden within the borders of the land of Canaan. But that law (as I have said) did not reach to any of those regions, however subjected unto the Jews, that were situated without those bounds.

Thus far concerning outward worship. Let us now consider articles of faith.

The articles of religion are some of them practical and some speculative. Now, though both sorts consist in the knowledge of truth, yet these terminate simply in the understanding, those influence the will and manners. Speculative opinions, therefore, and articles of faith (as they are called) which are required only to be believed, cannot be imposed on any church by the law of the land. For it is absurd that things should be enjoined by laws which are not in men's power to perform. And to believe this or that to be true, does not depend upon our will. But of this enough has been said already. But (will some say) let men at least profess that they believe. A sweet religion, indeed, that obliges men to dissemble and tell lies, both to God and man, for the salvation of their souls! If the magistrate thinks to save men thus, he seems to understand little of the way of salvation. And if he does it not in order to save them, why is he so solicitous about the articles of faith as to enact them by a law?

Further, the magistrate ought not to forbid the preaching or professing of any speculative opinions in any church, because they have no manner of relation to the civil rights of the subjects. If a Roman Catholic believe that to be really the body of Christ, which another man calls bread, he does no injury thereby to his neighbour. If a Jew do not believe the New Testament to be the word of God, he does not thereby alter anything in men's civil rights. If a heathen doubt of both Testaments, he is not therefore to be punished as a pernicious citizen. The power of the magistrate and the estates of the people may be equally secure whether any man believe these things or no. I readily grant that these opinions are false and absurd. But the business of laws is not to provide for the truth of opinions, but for the safety and security of the commonwealth, and of every particular man's goods and person. And so it ought to be. For the truth certainly would do well enough if she were once left to shift for herself. She seldom has received, and I fear never will receive, much assistance from the power of great men, to whom she is but rarely known, and more rarely welcome. She is not taught by laws, nor has she any need of force to procure her entrance into the minds of men. Errors indeed prevail by the assistance of foreign and borrowed succours. But if truth makes not her way into the understanding by her own light, she will be but the weaker for any borrowed force violence can add to her. Thus much for speculative opinions. Let us now proceed to practical ones.

A good life, in which consists not the least part of religion and true piety, concerns also the civil government; and in it lies the safety both of men's souls and of the commonwealth. Moral actions belong therefore to the jurisdiction both of the outward and inward court; both of the civil and domestic governor; I mean both of the magistrate and conscience. Here, therefore, is great danger, lest one of these jurisdictions intrench upon the other, and discord arise between the keeper of the public peace and the overseers of souls. But if what has been already said concerning the limits of both these governments be rightly considered, it will easily remove all difficulty in this matter.

Every man has an immortal soul, capable of eternal happiness or misery; whose happiness depending upon his believing and doing those things in this life which are necessary to the obtaining of God's favour, and are prescribed by God to that end. It follows from thence, first, that the observance of these things is the highest obligation that lies upon mankind, and that our utmost care, application, and diligence ought to be exercised in the search and performance of them; because there is nothing in this world that is of any consideration in comparison with eternity. Secondly, that seeing one man does not violate the right of another by his erroneous opinions and undue manner of worship, nor is his perdition any prejudice to another man's affairs, therefore, the care of each man's salvation belongs only to himself. But I would not have this understood as if I meant hereby to condemn all charitable admonitions, and affectionate endeavours to reduce men from errors, which are indeed the greatest duty of a Christian. Any one may employ as many exhortations and arguments as he pleases, towards the promoting of another man's salvation. But all force and compulsion are to be forborne. Nothing is to be done imperiously. Nobody is obliged in that matter to yield obedience unto the admonitions or injunctions of another, further than he himself is persuaded. Every man in that has the supreme and absolute authority of judging for himself. And the reason is because nobody else is concerned in it, nor can receive any prejudice from his conduct therein.

But besides their souls, which are immortal, men have also their temporal lives here upon earth; the state whereof being frail and fleeting, and the duration uncertain, they have need of several outward conveniencies to the support thereof, which are to be procured or preserved by pains and industry. For those things that are necessary to the comfortable support of our lives are not the spontaneous products of nature, nor do offer themselves fit and prepared for our use. This part therefore draws on another care, and necessarily gives another employment. But the pravity of mankind being such that they had rather injuriously prey upon the fruits of other men's labours than take pains to provide for themselves, the necessity of preserving men in the possession of what honest industry has already acquired, and also of preserving their liberty and strength, whereby they may acquire what they farther want, obliges men to enter into society with one another, that by mutual assistance and joint force they may secure unto each other their properties, in the things that contribute to the comfort and happiness of this life, leaving in the meanwhile to every man the care of his own eternal happiness, the attainment whereof can neither be facilitated by another man's industry, nor can the loss of it turn to another man's prejudice, nor the hope of it be forced from him by any external violence. But, forasmuch as men thus entering into societies, grounded upon their mutual compacts of assistance for the defence of their temporal goods, may, nevertheless, be deprived of them, either by the rapine and fraud of their fellow citizens, or by the hostile violence of foreigners, the remedy of this evil consists in arms, riches, and multitudes of citizens; the remedy of the other in laws; and the care of all things relating both to one and the other is committed by the society to the civil magistrate. This is the original, this is the use, and these are the bounds of the legislative (which is the supreme) power in every commonwealth. I mean, that provision may be made for the security of each man's private possessions; for the peace, riches, and public commodities of the whole people; and, as much as possible, for the increase of their inward strength against foreign invasions.

These things being thus explained, it is easy to understand to what end the legislative power ought to be directed, and by what measures regulated; and that is the temporal good and outward prosperity of the society; which is the sole reason of men's entering into society, and the only thing they seek and aim at in it. And it is also evident what liberty remains to men in reference to their eternal salvation, and that is, that every one should do what he in his conscience is persuaded to be acceptable to the Almighty, on whose good pleasure and acceptance depends their eternal happiness. For obedience is due, in the first place, to God, and afterwards to the laws.

But some may ask, What if the magistrate should enjoin anything by his authority that appears unlawful to the conscience of a private person? I answer, that if government be faithfully administered, and the counsels of the magistrates be indeed directed to the public good, this will seldom happen. But if, perhaps, it do so fall out, I say, that such a private person is to abstain from the action that he judges unlawful, and he is to undergo the punishment which it is not unlawful for him to bear. For the private judgment of any person concerning a law enacted in political matters, for the public good, does not take away the obligation of that law, nor deserve a dispensation. But if the law indeed be concerning things that lie not within the verge of the magistrate's authority (as for example, that the people, or any party amongst them, should be compelled to embrace a strange religion, and join in the worship and ceremonies of another church), men are not in these cases obliged by that law, against their consciences. For the political society is instituted for no other end, but only to secure every man's possession of the things of this life. The care of each man's soul, and of the things of heaven, which neither does belong to the commonwealth nor can be subjected to it, is left entirely to every man's self. Thus the safeguard of men's lives, and of the things that belong unto this life, is the business of the commonwealth; and the preserving of those things unto their owners is the duty of the magistrate. And therefore the magistrate cannot take away these worldly things from this man or party, and give them to that; nor change propriety amongst fellow-subjects (no not even by a law), for a cause that has no relation to the end of civil government, I mean for their religion, which whether it be true or false does no prejudice to the worldly concerns of their fellow-subjects, which are the things that only belong unto the care of the commonwealth.

But what if the magistrate believe such a law as this to be for the public good? I answer: as the private judgment of any particular person, if erroneous, does not exempt him from the obligation of law, so the private judgment (as I may call it) of the magistrate does not give him any new right of imposing laws upon his subjects, which neither was in the constitution of the government granted him, nor ever was in the power of the people to grant, much less if he make it his business to enrich and advance his followers and fellow-sectaries with the spoils of others. But what if the magistrate believe that he has a right to make such laws, and that they are for the public good? and his subjects believe the contrary? Who shall be judge between them? I answer, God alone. For there is no judge upon earth between the supreme magistrate and the people. God, I say, is the only judge in this case, who will retribute unto every one at the last day according to his deserts; that is, according to his sincerity and uprightness in endeavouring to promote piety, and the public weal and peace of mankind. But what shall be done in the meanwhile? I answer: The principal and chief care of every one ought to be of his own soul first, and, in the next place, of the public peace; though yet there are very few will think it is peace there, where they see all laid waste.

There are two sorts of contests amongst men, the one managed by law, the other by force; and these are of that nature that where the one ends, the other always begins. But it is not my business to inquire into the power of the magistrate in the different constitutions of nations. I only know what usually happens where controversies arise without a judge to determine them. You will say, then, the magistrate being the stronger will have his will, and carry his point. Without doubt; but the question is not here concerning the doubtfulness of the event, but the rule of right.

But to come to particulars. I say, first, no opinions contrary to human society, or to those moral rules which are necessary to the preservation of civil society, are to be tolerated by the magistrate. But of these, indeed, examples in any church are rare. For no sect can easily arrive to such a degree of madness as that it should think fit to teach, for doctrines of religion, such things as manifestly undermine the foundations of society, and are, therefore, condemned by the judgment of all mankind; because their own interest, peace, reputation, everything would be thereby endangered.

Another more secret evil, but more dangerous to the commonwealth, is when men arrogate to themselves, and to those of their own sect, some peculiar prerogative covered over with a specious show of deceitful words, but in effect opposite to the civil right of the community. For example: we cannot find any sect that teaches, expressly and openly, that men are not obliged to keep their promise; that princes may be dethroned by those that differ from them in religion; or that the dominion of all things belongs only to themselves. For these things, proposed thus nakedly and plainly, would soon draw on them the eye and hand of the magistrate, and awaken all the care of the commonwealth to a watchfulness against the spreading of so dangerous an evil. But, nevertheless, we find those that say the same things in other words. What else do they mean, who teach that faith is not to be kept with heretics? Their meaning, forsooth, is that the privilege of breaking faith belongs unto themselves; for they declare all that are not of their communion to be heretics, or at least may declare them so whensoever they think fit. What can be the meaning of their asserting that kings excommunicated forfeit their crowns and kingdoms? It is evident that they thereby arrogate unto themselves the power of deposing kings, because they challenge the power of excommunication, as the peculiar right of their hierarchy. That dominion is founded in grace is also an assertion by which those that maintain it do plainly lay claim to the possession of all things. For they are not so wanting to themselves as not to believe, or at least as not to profess themselves to be the truly pious and faithful. These therefore, and the like, who attribute unto the faithful, religious, and orthodox, that is, in plain terms, unto themselves, any peculiar privilege or power above other mortals, in civil concernments; or who upon pretence of religion do challenge any manner of authority over such as are not associated with them in their ecclesiastical communion, I say these have no right to be tolerated by the magistrate; as neither those that will not own and teach the duty of tolerating all men in matters of mere religion. For what do all these and the like doctrines signify, but that they may, and are ready upon any occasion to seize the government, and possess themselves of the estates and fortunes of their fellow-subjects; and that they only ask leave to be tolerated by the magistrate so long until they find themselves strong enough to effect it?

Again: That church can have no right to be tolerated by the magistrate which is constituted upon such a bottom that all those who enter into it do thereby *ipso facto* deliver themselves up to the protection and service of another prince. For by this means the magistrate would give way to the settling of a foreign jurisdiction in his own country, and suffer his own people to be listed, as it were, for soldiers against his own government. Nor does the frivolous and fallacious distinction between the court and the church afford any remedy to this inconvenience; especially when both the one and the other are equally subject to the absolute authority of the same person, who has not only power to persuade the members of his church to whatsoever he lists, either as purely religious, or in order thereunto, but can also enjoin it them on pain of eternal fire. It is ridiculous for any one to profess himself to be a Mahometan only in his religion, but in everything else a faithful subject to a Christian magistrate, whilst at the same time he acknowledges himself bound to yield blind obedience to the Mufti of Constantinople, who himself is entirely obedient to the Ottoman Emperor, and frames the feigned oracles of that religion according to his pleasure. But this Mahometan living amongst Christians would yet more apparently renounce their government if he acknowledged the same person to be head of his church who is the supreme magistrate in the state.

Lastly, those are not at all to be tolerated who deny the being of a God. Promises, covenants, and oaths, which are the bonds of human society, can have no hold upon an atheist. The taking away of God, though but even in thought, dissolves all; besides also, those that by their atheism undermine and destroy all religion, can have no pretence of religion whereupon to challenge the privilege of a toleration. As for other practical opinions, though not absolutely free from all error, if they do not tend to establish domination over others, or civil impunity to the church in which they are taught, there can be no reason why they should not be tolerated.

It remains that I say something concerning those assemblies which being vulgarly called, and perhaps having sometimes been conventicles and nurseries of factions and seditions, are thought to afford the strongest matter of objection against this doctrine of toleration. But this has not happened by anything peculiar unto the genius of such assemblies, but by the unhappy circumstances of an oppressed or ill-settled liberty. These accusations would soon cease if the law of toleration were once so settled that all churches were obliged to lay down toleration as the foundation of their own liberty, and teach that liberty of conscience is every man's natural right, equally belonging to dissenters as to themselves; and that nobody ought to be compelled in matters of religion either by law or force. The establishment of this one thing would take away all ground of complaints and tumults upon account of conscience; and these causes of discontents and animosities being once removed, there would remain nothing in these assemblies that were not more peaceable and less apt to produce disturbance of state than in any other meetings whatsoever. But let us examine particularly the heads of these accusations.

You will say that assemblies and meetings endanger the public peace, and threaten the commonwealth. I answer, if this be so, why are there daily such numerous meetings in markets and courts of judicature? Why are crowds upon the exchange, and a concourse of people in cities suffered? You will reply, those are civil assemblies, but these we object against are ecclesiastical. I answer, it is a likely thing indeed, that such assemblies as are altogether remote from civil affairs should be most apt to embroil them. Oh, but civil assemblies are composed of men that differ from one another in matters of religion, but these ecclesiastical meetings are of persons that are all of one opinion. As if an agreement in matters of religion were in effect a conspiracy against the commonwealth; or as if men would not be so much the more warmly unanimous in religion the less liberty they had of assembling. But it will be urged still, that civil assemblies are open and free for any one to enter into, whereas religious conventicles are more private, and thereby give opportunity to clandestine machinations. I answer, that this is not strictly true, for many civil assemblies are not open to every one. And if some religious meetings be private, who are they (I beseech you) that are to be blamed for it, those that desire, or those that forbid their being public? Again, you will say that religious communion does exceedingly unite men's minds and affections to one another, and is therefore the more dangerous. But if this be so, why is not the magistrate afraid of his own church; and why does he not forbid their assemblies as things dangerous to his government? You will say because he himself is a part, and even the head of them. As if he were not also a part of the commonwealth, and the head of the whole people!

Let us therefore deal plainly. The magistrate is afraid of other churches, but not of his own; because he is kind and favourable to the one, but severe and cruel to the other. These he treats like children, and indulges them even to wantonness. Those he uses as slaves, and how blamelessly soever they demean themselves, recompenses them no otherwise than by galleys, prisons, confiscations, and death. These he cherishes and defends; those he continually scourges and oppresses. Let him turn the tables. Or let those dissenters enjoy but the same privileges in civils as his other subjects, and he will quickly find that these religious meetings will be no longer dangerous. For if men enter into seditious conspiracies, it is not religion inspires them to it in their meetings, but their sufferings and oppressions that make them willing to ease themselves. Just and moderate governments are everywhere quiet, everywhere safe; but oppression raises ferments and makes men struggle to cast off an uneasy and tyrannical yoke. I know that seditions are very frequently raised upon pretence of religion, but it is as true that for religion subjects are frequently ill treated, and live miserably. Believe me, the stirs that are made proceed not from any peculiar temper of this or that church or religious society, but from the common disposition of all mankind, who when they groan under any heavy burthen endeavour naturally to shake off the yoke that galls their necks. Suppose this business of religion were let alone, and that there were some other distinction made between men and men upon account of their different complexions, shapes, and features, so that those who have black hair (for example) or grey eyes should not enjoy the same privileges as other citizens; that they should not be permitted either to buy or sell, or live by their callings; that parents should not have the government and education of their own children; that all should either be excluded from the benefit of the laws, or meet with partial judges; can it be doubted but these persons, thus distinguished from others by the colour of their hair and eyes, and united together by one common persecution, would be as dangerous to the magistrate as any others that had associated themselves merely upon the account of religion? Some enter into company for trade and profit, others for want of business have their clubs for claret. Neighbourhood joins some, and religion others. But there is only one thing which gathers people into seditious commotions, and that is oppression.

You will say, What, will you have people to meet at divine service against the magistrate's will? I answer, Why, I pray, against his will? Is it not both lawful and necessary that they should meet? Against his will, do you say? That is what I complain of; that is the very root of all the mischief. Why are assemblies less sufferable in a church than in a theatre or market? Those that meet there are not either more vicious or more turbulent than those that meet elsewhere. The business in that is that they are ill used, and therefore they are not to be suffered. Take away the partiality that is used towards them in matters of common right; change the laws, take away the penalties unto which they are subjected, and all things will immediately become safe and peaceable; nay, those that are averse to the religion of the magistrate will think themselves so much the more bound to maintain the peace of the commonwealth as their condition is better in that place than elsewhere; and all the several separate congregations, like so many guardians of the public peace, will watch one another, that nothing may be innovated or changed in the form of the government, because they can hope for nothing better than what they already enjoy—that is, an equal condition with their fellow-subjects under a just and moderate government. Now if that church which agrees in religion with the prince be esteemed the chief support of any civil government, and that for no other reason (as has already been shewn) than because the prince is kind and the laws are favourable to it, how much greater will be the security of government where all good subjects, of whatsoever church they be, without any distinction upon account of religion, enjoying the same favour of the prince and the same benefit of the laws, shall become the common support and guard of it, and where none will have any occasion to fear the severity of the laws but those that do injuries to their neighbours and offend against the civil peace?

That we may draw towards a conclusion. The sum of all we drive at is that every man may enjoy the same rights that are granted to others. Is it permitted to worship God in the Roman manner? Let it be permitted to do it in the Geneva form also. Is it permitted to speak Latin in the market-place? Let those that have a mind to it be permitted to do it also in the church. Is it lawful for any man in his own house to kneel, stand, sit, or use any other posture; and to clothe himself in white or black, in short or in long garments? Let it not be made unlawful to eat bread, drink wine, or wash with water in the church. In a word, whatsoever things are left free by law in the common occasions of life, let them remain free unto every church in divine worship. Let no man's life, or body, or house, or estate, suffer any manner of prejudice upon these accounts. Can you allow of the Presbyterian discipline? Why should not the Episcopal also have what they like? Ecclesiastical authority, whether it be administered by the hands of a single person or many, is everywhere the same; and neither has any jurisdiction in things civil, nor any manner of power of compulsion, nor anything at all to do with riches and revenues.

Ecclesiastical assemblies and sermons are justified by daily experience and public allowance. These are allowed to people of some one persuasion, why not to all? If anything pass in a religious meeting seditiously and contrary to the public peace, it is to be punished in the same manner, and no otherwise than as if it had happened in a fair or market. These meetings ought not to be sanctuaries for factious and flagitious fellows. Nor ought it to be less lawful for men to meet in churches than in halls; nor are one part of the subjects to be esteemed more blameable for their meeting together than others. Every one is to be accountable for his own actions, and no man is to be laid under a suspicion or odium for the fault of another. Those that are seditious, murderers, thieves, robbers, adulterers, slanderers, etc., of whatsoever church, whether national or not, ought to be punished and suppressed. But those whose doctrine is peaceable, and whose manners are pure and blameless, ought to be upon equal terms with their fellow-subjects. Thus if solemn assemblies, observations of festivals, public worship be permitted to any one sort of professors, all these things ought to be permitted to the Presbyterians, Independents, Anabaptists, Arminians, Quakers, and others, with the same liberty. Nay, if we may openly speak the truth, and as becomes one man to another, neither Pagan nor Mahometan, nor Jew, ought to be excluded from the civil rights of the commonwealth because of his religion. The Gospel commands no such thing. The church which "judgeth not those that are without" (1 Cor. v. 12, 13) wants it not. And the commonwealth, which embraces indifferently all men that are honest, peaceable, and industrious, requires it not. Shall we suffer a Pagan to deal and trade with us, and shall we not suffer him to pray unto and worship God? If we allow the Jews to have private houses and dwellings amongst us, why should we not allow them to have synagogues? Is their doctrine more false, their worship more abominable, or is the civil peace more endangered by their meeting in public than in their private houses? But if these things may be granted to Jews and Pagans, surely the condition of any Christians ought not to be worse than theirs in a Christian commonwealth.

You will say, perhaps, Yes, it ought to be; because they are more inclinable to factions, tumults, and civil wars. I answer, Is this the fault of the Christian religion? If it be so, truly the Christian religion is the worst of all religions, and ought neither to be embraced by any particular person, nor tolerated by any commonwealth. For if this be the genius, this the nature of the Christian religion, to be turbulent, and destructive to the civil peace, that church itself which the magistrate indulges will not always be innocent. But far be it from us to say any such thing of that religion which carries the greatest opposition to covetousness, ambition, discord, contention, and all manner of inordinate desires; and is the most modest and peaceable religion that ever was. We must therefore seek another cause of those evils that are charged upon religion. And if we consider right, we shall find it to consist wholly in the subject that I am treating of. It is not the diversity of opinions (which cannot be avoided), but the refusal of toleration to those that are of different opinions (which might have been granted), that has produced all the bustles and wars that have been in the Christian world upon account of religion. The heads and leaders of the church, moved by avarice and insatiable desire of dominion, making use of the immoderate ambition of magistrates and the credulous superstition of the giddy multitude, have incensed and animated them against those that dissent from themselves, by preaching unto them, contrary to the laws of the Gospel and to the precepts of charity, that schismatics and heretics are to be outed of their possessions and destroyed. And thus have they mixed together and confounded two things that are in themselves most different, the church and the commonwealth. Now as it is very difficult for men patiently to suffer themselves to be stripped of the goods which they have got by their honest industry, and, contrary to all the laws of equity, both human and divine, to be delivered up for a prey to other men's violence and rapine; especially when they are otherwise altogether blameless; and that the occasion for which they are thus treated does not at all belong to the jurisdiction of the magistrate, but entirely to the conscience of every particular man, for the conduct of which he is accountable to God only; what else can be expected but that these men, growing weary of the evils under which they labour, should in the end think it lawful for them to resist force with force, and to defend their natural rights (which are not forfeitable upon account of religion) with arms as well as they can? That this has been hitherto the ordinary course of things is abundantly evident in history, and that it will continue to be so hereafter is but too apparent in reason. It cannot, indeed, be otherwise so long as the principle of persecution for religion shall prevail, as it has done hitherto, with magistrate and people, and so long as those that ought to be the preachers of peace and concord shall continue with all their art and strength to excite men to arms and sound the trumpet of war. But that magistrates should thus suffer these incendiaries and disturbers of the public peace might justly be wondered at if it did not appear that they have been invited by them unto a participation of the spoil, and have therefore thought fit to make use of their covetousness and pride as means whereby to increase their own power. For who does not see that these good men are indeed more ministers of the government than ministers of the Gospel, and that by flattering the ambition and favouring the dominion of princes and men in authority, they endeavour with all their might to promote that tyranny in the commonwealth which otherwise they should not be able to establish in the church? This is the unhappy agreement that we see between the church and state. Whereas if each of them would contain itself within its own bounds—the one attending to the worldly welfare of the commonwealth, the other to the salvation of souls—it is impossible that any discord should ever have happened between them. *Sed pudet hæc opprobria, etc.* God Almighty grant, I beseech him, that the gospel of peace may at length be preached, and that civil magistrates, growing more careful to conform their own consciences to the law of God and less solicitous about the binding of other men's consciences by human laws, may, like fathers of their country, direct all their counsels and endeavours to promote universally the civil welfare of all their children, except only of such as are arrogant, ungovernable, and injurious to their brethren; and that all ecclesiastical men, who boast themselves to be the successors of the apostles, walking peaceably and modestly in the apostles' steps, without intermeddling with state affairs, may apply themselves wholly to promote the salvation of souls.

FAREWELL.

Perhaps it may not be amiss to add a few things concerning heresy and schism. A Turk is not, nor can be, either heretic or schismatic to a Christian; and if any man fall off from the Christian faith to Mahometism, he does not thereby become a heretic or schismatic, but an apostate and an infidel. This nobody doubts of; and by this it appears that men of different religions cannot be heretics or schismatics to one another.

We are to inquire therefore what men are of the same religion. Concerning which it is manifest that those who have one and the same rule of faith and worship are of the same religion; and those who have not the same rule of faith and worship are of different religions. For since all things that belong unto that religion are contained in that rule, it follows necessarily that those who agree in one rule are of one and the same religion, and *vice versâ*. Thus Turks and Christians are of different religions, because these take the Holy Scriptures to be the rule of their religion, and those the Alcoran. And for the same reason there may be different religions also even amongst Christians. The Papists and Lutherans, though both of them profess faith in Christ, and are therefore called Christians, yet are not both of the same religion, because these acknowledge nothing but the Holy Scriptures to be the rule and foundation of their religion, those take in also traditions and the decrees of popes, and of these together make the rule of their religion; and thus the Christians of St. John (as they are called) and the Christians of Geneva are of different religions, because these also take only the Scriptures, and those I know not what traditions, for the rule of their religion.

This being settled, it follows, first, that heresy is a separation made in ecclesiastical communion between men of the same religion for some opinions no way contained in the rule itself; and, secondly, that amongst those who acknowledge nothing but the Holy Scriptures to be their rule of faith, heresy is a separation made in their Christian communion for opinions not contained in the express words of Scripture. Now this separation may be made in a twofold manner:—

1. When the greater part, or by the magistrate's patronage the stronger part, of the church separates itself from others by excluding them out of her communion because they will not profess their belief of certain opinions which are not the express words of the Scripture. For it is not the paucity of those that are separated, nor the authority of the magistrate, that can make any man guilty of heresy, but he only is a heretic who divides the church into parts, introduces names and marks of distinction, and voluntarily makes a separation because of such opinions.

2. When any one separates himself from the communion of a church because that church does not publicly profess some certain opinions which the Holy Scriptures do not expressly teach.

Both these are heretics because they err in fundamentals, and they err obstinately against knowledge; for when they have determined the Holy Scriptures to be the only foundation of faith, they nevertheless lay down certain propositions as fundamental which are not in the Scripture, and because others will not acknowledge these additional opinions of theirs, nor build upon them as if they were necessary and fundamental, they therefore make a separation in the church, either by withdrawing themselves from others, or expelling the others from them. Nor does it signify anything for them to say that their confessions and symbols are agreeable to Scripture and to the analogy of faith; for if they be conceived in the express words of Scripture, there can be no question about them, because those things are acknowledged by all Christians to be of divine inspiration, and therefore fundamental. But if they say that the articles which they require to be professed are consequences deduced from the Scripture, it is undoubtedly well done of them who believe and profess such things as seem unto them so agreeable to the rule of faith. But it would be very ill done to obtrude those things upon others unto whom they do not seem to be the indubitable doctrines of the Scripture; and to make a separation for such things as these, which neither are nor can be fundamental, is to become heretics; for I do not think there is any man arrived to that degree of madness as that he dare give out his consequences and interpretations of Scripture as divine inspirations, and compare the articles of faith that he has framed according to his own fancy with the authority of Scripture. I know there are some propositions so evidently agreeable to Scripture that nobody can deny them to be drawn from thence, but about those, therefore, there can be no difference. This only I say—that however clearly we may think this or the other doctrine to be deduced from Scripture, we ought not therefore to impose it upon others as a necessary article of faith because we believe it to be agreeable to the rule of faith, unless we would be content also that other doctrines should be imposed upon us in the same manner, and that we should be compelled to receive and profess all the different and contradictory opinions of Lutherans, Calvinists, Remonstrants, Anabaptists, and other sects which the contrivers of symbols, systems, and confessions are accustomed to deliver to their followers as genuine and necessary deductions from the Holy Scripture. I cannot but wonder at the extravagant arrogance of those men who think that they themselves can explain things necessary to salvation more clearly than the Holy Ghost, the eternal and infinite wisdom of God.

Thus much concerning heresy, which word in common use is applied only to the doctrinal part of religion. Let us now consider schism, which is a crime near akin to it; for both these words seem unto me to signify an ill-grounded separation in ecclesiastical communion made about things not necessary. But since use, which is the supreme law in matter of language, has determined that heresy relates to errors in faith, and schism to those in worship or discipline, we must consider them under that distinction.

Schism, then, for the same reasons that have already been alleged, is nothing else but a separation made in the communion of the church upon account of something in divine worship or ecclesiastical discipline that is not any necessary part of it. Now, nothing in worship or discipline can be necessary to Christian communion but what Christ our legislator, or the apostles by inspiration of the Holy Spirit, have commanded in express words.

In a word, he that denies not anything that the Holy Scriptures teach in express words, nor makes a separation upon occasion of anything that is not manifestly contained in the sacred text—however he may be nicknamed by any sect of Christians, and declared by some or all of them to be utterly void of true Christianity—yet in deed and in truth this man cannot be either a heretic or schismatic.

These things might have been explained more largely and more advantageously, but it is enough to have hinted at them thus briefly to a person of your parts.

DOVER·THRIFT·EDITIONS

FICTION

THE QUEEN OF SPADES AND OTHER STORIES, Alexander Pushkin. 128pp. 0-486-28054-3

THE STORY OF AN AFRICAN FARM, Olive Schreiner. 256pp. 0-486-40165-0

FRANKENSTEIN, Mary Shelley. 176pp. 0-486-28211-2

THE JUNGLE, Upton Sinclair. 320pp. (Available in U.S. only.) 0-486-41923-1

THREE LIVES, Gertrude Stein. 176pp. (Available in U.S. only.) 0-486-28059-4

THE BODY SNATCHER AND OTHER TALES, Robert Louis Stevenson. 80pp. 0-486-41924-X

THE STRANGE CASE OF DR. JEKYLL AND MR. HYDE, Robert Louis Stevenson. 64pp. 0-486-26688-5

TREASURE ISLAND, Robert Louis Stevenson. 160pp. 0-486-27559-0

GULLIVER'S TRAVELS, Jonathan Swift. 240pp. 0-486-29273-8

THE KREUTZER SONATA AND OTHER SHORT STORIES, Leo Tolstoy. 144pp. 0-486-27805-0

THE WARDEN, Anthony Trollope. 176pp. 0-486-40076-X

FATHERS AND SONS, Ivan Turgenev. 176pp. 0-486-40073-5

ADVENTURES OF HUCKLEBERRY FINN, Mark Twain. 224pp. 0-486-28061-6

THE ADVENTURES OF TOM SAWYER, Mark Twain. 192pp. 0-486-40077-8

THE MYSTERIOUS STRANGER AND OTHER STORIES, Mark Twain. 128pp. 0-486-27069-6

HUMOROUS STORIES AND SKETCHES, Mark Twain. 80pp. 0-486-29279-7

AROUND THE WORLD IN EIGHTY DAYS, Jules Verne. 160pp. 0-486-41111-7

CANDIDE, Voltaire (François-Marie Arouet). 112pp. 0-486-26689-3

GREAT SHORT STORIES BY AMERICAN WOMEN, Candace Ward (ed.). 192pp. 0-486-28776-9

"THE COUNTRY OF THE BLIND" AND OTHER SCIENCE-FICTION STORIES, H. G. Wells. 160pp. (Not available in Europe or United Kingdom.) 0-486-29569-9

THE ISLAND OF DR. MOREAU, H. G. Wells. 112pp. (Not available in Europe or United Kingdom.) 0-486-29027-1

THE INVISIBLE MAN, H. G. Wells. 112pp. (Not available in Europe or United Kingdom.) 0-486-27071-8

THE TIME MACHINE, H. G. Wells. 80pp. (Not available in Europe or United Kingdom.) 0-486-28472-7

THE WAR OF THE WORLDS, H. G. Wells. 160pp. (Not available in Europe or United Kingdom.) 0-486-29506-0

ETHAN FROME, Edith Wharton. 96pp. 0-486-26690-7

SHORT STORIES, Edith Wharton. 128pp. 0-486-28235-X

THE AGE OF INNOCENCE, Edith Wharton. 288pp. 0-486-29803-5

THE PICTURE OF DORIAN GRAY, Oscar Wilde. 192pp. 0-486-27807-7

JACOB'S ROOM, Virginia Woolf. 144pp. (Not available in Europe or United Kingdom.) 0-486-40109-X